Our Newlywed
KITCHEN

Dear Gift-giver,

An engagement, shower, or wedding calls for a special gift.

Our Newlywed Kitchen is that and more as you create a keepsake by

adding your personal touch. Encourage and inspire the new couple

by adding a prayer or offer of best wishes, wisdom learned from

your own enduring marriage, trusted family recipes, and

time-honored traditions. Let your handwritten messages

continue to bless them for years to come.

Pages to Personalize

Our Newlywed KITCHEN

The Art of Cooking, Gathering, and Creating Traditions

Laura Schupp

WITH

Love

FROM

Mom & Dad

DATE

July / 17 / 2018

As you begin to build your
marriage and your new home
together, may you cherish
your togetherness when you
create and eat healthy
and delicious food in your
kitchen. Enjoy!

Friends & family
Chime in...

With blessings, best wishes, & good advice

from

from

from

from

from

....
....
....
....
....
....

from

....
....
....
....
....
....

from

....
....
....
....
....
....

from

....
....
....
....
....
....

from

....
....
....
....
....
....

from

....
....
....
....
....
....

Our Newlywed Kitchen: The Art of Cooking, Gathering, and Creating Traditions
© 2018 Laura Schupp

A Focus on the Family book published by Tyndale House Publishers, Inc., Carol Stream, Illinois 60188

Focus on the Family and the accompanying logo and design are federally registered trademarks of
Focus on the Family, 8605 Explorer Drive, Colorado Springs, CO 80920.

TYNDALE and Tyndale's quill logo are registered trademarks of Tyndale House Publishers, Inc.

Interior design by CanOpener Creative
Cover design by Eva Winters
Shutterstock, iStockPhoto (photo credits page 220)
Cover photograph of forks copyright © gvinpin/Getty Images. All rights reserved.
Cover photograph of tomatoes copyright © Jacek Chabraszewski/Adobe Stock. All rights reserved.
Cover illustration of fork and knife copyright © by Adèle Foucart/Noun Project. All rights reserved.
Cover illustration of plate and spoon by Eva Winters. Copyright © Tyndale House Publishers, Inc. All rights reserved.
Cover photograph of spaghetti swirl copyright © Melica/Adobe Stock. All rights reserved.
Photos on pages 12, 28, 62, 64, 93, 195, and 208 are from the personal collection of the author and are used by permission.

For information about special discounts for bulk purchases, please contact Tyndale House Publishers at
csresponse@tyndale.com, or call 1-800-323-9400.

Library of Congress Cataloging-in-Publication Data can be found at www.loc.gov.
ISBN 978-1-58997-945-1

Printed in China

24 23 22 21 20 19 18
7 6 5 4 3 2 1

Teach the bride, and forever change the family

First and foremost, to my heavenly Father, who provided the words, opened and closed doors, and further strengthened my trust in Him.

To my husband, Thom, who loves to share the kitchen with me and continually supports my lofty endeavors.

To my daughter, Elise, and niece, Alex, and to every bride seeking to nourish and nurture through the heart of her home.

To Bob, who championed this project, and to Julie, who shepherded it well.

CONTENTS

AUTHOR'S NOTE

Our Newlywed Kitchen is a mother's notes to her daughter. It's a conversation between an encouraging mentor and you, the beautiful bride. It's a guide, a planner, and a tutorial that will equip you to build a loving and nurturing home, all by bringing the basic elements of the kitchen together. Simply put:

....

I want to challenge you to change lives through the heart of the home—your kitchen.

....

Don't worry, this book will not return you to an era of outdated ideals. Rather, it illustrates how to cultivate the timeless value of gathering friends and family to your table while mixing in today's emphasis on healthy, simple food and contemporary solutions. The skills you'll uncover in this book have the power to bless generations to come.

Here's wishing you a lifetime of happiness together.

Laura

This is an exciting time for both of you.

You have found your special someone and chosen to build a future together. Enjoy your new beginning to the fullest! As you already know, this is also a time for decisions. Along with all the immediate choices concerning your wedding day celebration—your dress, the venue, the honeymoon destination—you are also deciding where you will live, with possible career changes and relocations to consider as well. You have a lot on your plate, but this book is not meant to overwhelm you. First, read my advice for selecting the perfect wedding registry, and then come back to the rest as you settle into your new home. You'll find concepts I hope you'll enjoy for the rest of your life. After all, we need food—and love—every day. Why not learn how to connect these necessities? I'm happy to share with you what I've learned—from setting an inviting table and hosting a gathering, to creating a lifetime of togetherness.

Congrats to your lucky guy, too! Look for occasions to take "mental snapshots" during this special time. Trust me, these moments are fleeting and you'll cherish the memories.

Our Newlywed
KITCHEN

• CULTURAL SHIFT •

Cultural Shift

I believe your generation is in the midst of a cultural change, one emphasizing hearth and home. And I'm curious, are you seeing it too? As women, the definition of our roles has certainly shifted from one extreme to the other, moving away from domesticity toward careers and back again. As was the norm, many in my grandmother's generation didn't work outside the home. If they chose an occupational path, they were confronted by the challenges placed on them by society where discrimination was the norm. My mother, like many of her peers, held a full-time position, yet the bulk of the domestic duties still largely rested upon her shoulders.

Fast forward another 20 years to my generation—when women found themselves in an unpleasant divide between those who chose to work outside the home and those who didn't. The women who chose to combine children and careers were labeled "Super Moms." Looking back, I think many of us were so enamored with our widely accepted option to have a career, afforded to us by our brave predecessors who paved the way, that we became critical of those who didn't choose a similar path. Unfortunately, our critical attitude actually opposed what we said we were seeking—freedom.

Things of value never really go out of style.

The cultural changes in my generation specifically attacked the kitchen. Working moms with children found they struggled to find the time to cook, and many stay-at-home moms found themselves too busy with their children's events to spend much time in the kitchen. Enter the rising glut of fast food restaurants, pre-packaged meals, and boxed dinners—and the kitchen became easily abandoned. Who could blame my generation, really? We'd seen our mothers exhaustively try to do it all. So it's no wonder many of us didn't train your generation in the art of cooking. We thought we were doing you a favor by liberating you from the apron.

One of the benefits of maturity is witnessing the trends and cycles of life. For example, gold was popular the year of my wedding, evidenced by my ring, flatware, and even the rim on my crystal and china pattern. And now gold is back in fashion in a big way, because things of value never really go out of style. Like gold, preparing good food at home for friends and loved ones is timeless, and I'm happy to see your generation bringing it back into vogue.

I like the way your generation thinks. I know a bit about your mind-set because I've raised three of you. I've witnessed you renewing fashion trends of the past—wing tip boots and frilly aprons, for example—while the guys are sporting beards with handlebar mustaches. Many of you are into gardening, canning, and even knitting. A focus on personal health has led you to organic foods and exercise. I applaud you for holding on to the best of past generations as you seek what you feel you've missed, and at the same time putting your own unique influence on a work- and home-life balance—bringing authenticity to both. I am energized by this return to homemade and home-centric living via the kitchen. I've always found this room to be the setting for so many essential components of our daily life. The obvious reason for this hub of the home is the food we eat, but what we do in the kitchen also affects our fitness, finances, family, friendships and even our faith. In keeping with the alliteration, may I also add fun? This is where the two of you will cook, eat, gather, and pray, but also where you'll plan events, entertain guests, stay healthy, and save money.

My aim is to help you broaden your definition of a kitchen. Yes, the heart of your home can be the center of a healthy lifestyle, but it can also be a romantic space for the two of you.

Together, you can discover the blessings of your kitchen.

Starting today, you get to choose your path together. Take a close look at the current culture, and then take time to discuss the kind of marriage, lifestyle, and family you hope to build. You already have a picture in your mind—it's the reason you chose him, and he you. A strong bond and happy home doesn't just happen; it takes a plan, hard work, and a choice every day. What role will your kitchen play in your lifestyle? As you consider that, start thinking about your wedding registry. But before you drift off to happily scan coveted culinary tools, you may need a refresher on what's new and what's tried-and-true. *Our Newlywed Kitchen* will reveal the essential culinary tools for your registry. So get going, and fan the embers of the back-to-the-kitchen cultural shift.

No boundaries. A return to authentic living has found its way into our villages, big & small.

Our Newlywed

KITCHEN

• REGISTRY PRE-SHOP •

SOMETHING
BLUE

Showered with Love

I recently attended the bridal shower of one of my daughter's closest friends, Anna. It was such a blessed event with so much promise for two lives about to begin their journey together. This was a ladies gathering, mostly women in her mother's age group. I mention it to shed light on the wisdom in that room—wisdom about how to keep a marriage healthy, pure, and strong for the long haul. We opened with a prayer—my favorite part of the shower. Our hostess blessed us with her beautiful words. She prayed for the haven that Anna would create in the home she and her fiancé, William, would start together. She prayed that all of the beautiful gifts they would receive be used to bring comfort and hospitality to their home, and that their lives would be defined by peace, love, and unity. Finally, she prayed for the marriage they would begin to enjoy in just a few short weeks.

As I watched Anna open her shower gifts, I envisioned the thought and planning that went into each selected item on her registry: the turkey platter for the holidays, the pale blue salad plates that would add a touch of spring to Anna's table after the long winter, and the bright multi-colored bowl she intended for summer cookouts. She was thinking through the life she would share with William. She was imagining the fun, the love, the laughter—the celebrations that would shape their lives. It was incredibly romantic to witness. I was filled with hope—hope in the knowledge that there is still goodness, love, and excitement around building a life with each other.

As you consider your registry, look forward to the excitement of your wedding shower. That's when you'll see the pieces of your future home and life begin to become solid and real.

The Kitchen
you will create, learn in, & love

Walk into any store with a gift registry and at first glance you are bound to be wonderfully overwhelmed.

Yet before you say "I do," you may first find yourself asking:

- "Do I need both fine and casual dinnerware?"

- "Do I want eight, ten, or twelve place settings?"

- "Do I have space for multiple small appliances?"

The in-store registry lists will tell you what you supposedly need to fill your kitchen. Retailers will make all of their products look irresistible—and let's face it, that's their job. But what if you don't see the need for twelve place settings of fine dinnerware, crystal, and flatware? Or enough platters to serve a small army? You may ask yourself if these items are useful or necessary.

The next few pages will help you answer these questions. My hope is to shed light on why registering is still a good idea, while offering guidelines for you and your fiancé as you prepare for the registry. You'll also find the *Our Newlywed Kitchen Essentials Checklist*, which makes it easy to see what products will be useful for specific purposes in your kitchen. I've cut out the fluff, so you can have a clear vision of how items on your registry can work for you or be left off your list all together.

Please know that the list is only a template—a well-meaning set of recommendations. It's a conversation that began with my daughter and now extends to you. You'll find that sometimes we agree, and sometimes we agree to disagree. The point is to take time to think before you shop. That way, you'll avoid costly missteps and make the most educated choice for your particular needs. Registering is a well-thought-out celebration and plan for your life together, which should be stewarded wisely. But it's also a fun field trip with your betrothed. Enjoy the journey! This only happens once.

Honeymoon is to marriage as registry is to kitchen.

The honeymoon, as you are well aware, is the initial period of enthusiasm a newlywed couple experiences. Named in reference to the "waning of the moon," it is a reminder of this sweet but fleeting time in which this newness will last.

Just as there is a honeymoon time in your marriage, there is also a honeymoon period with your new kitchen, and it begins with your registry. While cooking every night or most nights may appear tedious, it doesn't have to be. Create a love relationship with your new kitchen now. Harness that enthusiasm during this precious sliver of time. I will revisit ideas on how to continually revive the "honeymoon" phase of your kitchen in future chapters, but I'll give you a little hint: it goes hand-in-hand with keeping your marriage fresh and alive, too.

Your registry is an opportunity to let the gift-givers gift well.

The Gifters
An Expression of Love

I've noticed the millennial bride seems focused on more practical items for her registry. I've learned your reasons are varied and valid. You are short on space, realistic about your future entertaining plans, or have witnessed elders and peers who have fine pieces but don't use them. I commend you on your pragmatism and really can't blame you for a utilitarian focus on the here and now. After all, you are entering a brand new stage of life, joining your life with another, and that's plenty to occupy your thoughts.

Even so, may I bend your ear for a moment and share some thoughts you may not have considered? My generation, many of whom will be your gift-givers, want to buy you what you want, which is why we shop off of your registry. But we also long to give you a keepsake. We see your marriage as lasting, and we want our gift to be a beautiful contribution to your new home that will span the years. Truth be told, many of us hope to be remembered fondly by our gift as you use it throughout the years.

The necessities will always take care of themselves.

You will always find disposable income for the disposable items: shower curtains, bed sheets, pizza cutter, or clothes hamper. If you need it, you'll buy it. What you will find difficult to purchase for yourself—no matter your income level—is a beautiful serving tray, a pricey place setting, or elegant crystal candlesticks. There will always be other priorities for those dollars. While I know the necessities do have a place on your registry (I even authored a section for them), my hope is that you don't forgo the finer items.

Consider fine items as you finalize your choices.

Life won't always look like it does right now. Someday, the baton will be passed, and it will be your turn to set a holiday table and serve the turkey. On that note, if you choose to place some of the finer items on your registry, I hope you find opportunities to use them long before that day. It is our wish as gift-givers that you have many celebrations in your life together, and through our gifting, we hope to be a small part of each one.

It's a Date, not an Errand.

If we're honest with one another, I think you'll agree that some men may not be jumping at the chance to spend two to three hours of intensely focused time in the housewares section of a department store. This is where the gentle art of persuasion comes into play. Please don't hear trickery, deceit, or subterfuge in this message, but an opportunity to open his world to the culinary advantages he will experience as he accepts his role in co-building a home with you. Whether you place importance on great cuisine, healthy living, organized space, entertaining guests, or something else, your ideas will introduce him to your creative and nurturing spirit in an inviting way. The following *MyTips* will help you spin the event into a fun-loving adventure.

Allow your fiancé to surprise you with his interest and opinions as he embraces the task he may have been secretly dreading.

add the
fun!

THE REGISTRY DATE *MyTips*

Dress up: You are a gift to one another. Present yourself well for this occasion. By dressing up you are promising more fun to be had later, à la dinner and a movie.

Plan to dine before or after your registry meeting time. This strategy not only supports a date-like outing but also allows more time to talk over specifics or speed bumps while they are fresh on your minds.

Give yourselves ample time, approximately two to three hours, in two to three visits.

Do your homework first: Bring your notes with room for additional thoughts or questions to jot down during your shop. Don't forget color swatches or specific measurements you need to consider. If you sense reluctance on your fiancé's part, this is a good time to enlist his support. Ask him to do a little product research in one of the areas of great interest to him. Can't find one? Suggest cutlery, grilling essentials, or specific tools such as a pizza stone, immersion blender, or French press for the coffee connoisseur.

Take breaks as needed. If you feel overwhelmed, stop shopping and grab coffee or tea. Some time outside the store will help you realign your goals.

Energy: Both parties need to maintain an enthusiastic mood, a rested body, and an engaged approach.

Listen for clues: Respect each other's opinions and listen for "must haves." Both of you may have a fun story or fond childhood memory to share. Either way, it's an opportunity to learn more about each other.

Do-Overs are okay: If it's just not working, don't force it and let a negative moment taint what should be a sweet memory. Just plan for another time. Agree to come back and try again later.

Say "No" to guests: This is your marriage and your start as a couple. Savor and share your new beginning with each other.

Celebrate the moment: Take selfies and post them. It's a great way to hint where you're registered.

Takeaways from your first registry shop?

_____

_____

_____

_____

Why Register?

WHY NOT?

There are actually more good reasons to set up a registry than you might think. Let's take a look at some valuable takeaways:

Avoid duplication: A registry nearly eliminates the chance of ending up with duplicate gifts. I say *nearly,* because some people don't shop from the registry and retail registry mistakes can happen. Even so, your chances of ending up with two toasters are reduced by registering.

Make it easy on guests: A wide array of gifts offer a variation of price points to choose from, so select items in all price ranges to allow for all guest's budgets. On that same note, don't be afraid to put a pricey set of cookware on your registry, as a doting family member or group from work may clan together to buy it. While it's noble to aim for a smaller registry to avoid appearing pretentious, a sparse registry may put your last-minute, or more budget-conscious gift-givers at a disadvantage, forcing them to shop off-registry or opt for a gift card. Both are certainly viable, acceptable, and appreciated options, but your guests shouldn't feel as though there are fewer choices simply because they procrastinated or can't afford what's available.

Find the missing thank-you card: Should a gift be delivered without a card included, your store can track the name of the gifter from its registry database. Mishap averted.

Solve future gift problems: Most retailers will leave your registry open for two years, or longer if requested. This is a chance for family to fulfill your place settings through birthday, anniversary, and holiday gifting.

PRE-SHOP
HOMEWORK OUTING

By now you can probably tell that shopping for your registry is a little more than a quick errand. Instead, view this as the beginning of your new life as a couple, and aim for it to be a time of connection.

To take the pressure off, do a little pre-shop homework. Find some time to plot your space and research your options. You probably already know a bit about each other's tastes, style, and preferred color palette but if not, or if some melding needs to take place, try to find common ground before you hit the retailers.

First and foremost, include him in everything—after all, it's his kitchen and home, too. He may surprise you with his level of interest and how much he cares about the space you will create together. Sharing responsibility in the planning stages will tend to engage him later.

Set realistic goals: What are your expectations for the first visit? Have a game plan. Front-end load your shopping trip with the items that excite you most.

Place settings: 8, 10, 12? How many will you need? Think into the future a bit, and the size of your family, but also consider the size of your current dining table and storage spaces.

Choose a color palette together: Gravitate toward colors you like to wear. Be inspired by a favorite article of clothing or piece of art. What colors make you feel comfortable, alive, attractive? Do you both agree?

Fine vs. Casual Dinnerware: Should you register for one or the other? Or both? (See Page 62)

Registry Pre-Shop *MyTips*

Download a Pre-Shop Planner at OurNewlywedKitchen.com.

Set a budget: Where is your mutual budgetary comfort zone? Even though they will be gifts you receive, are you both comfortable with the price point of those gifts? Will your guests be able to afford them? What if you have to pay for the remaining registry items yourself to complete a set of dishes?

Think space: Too many items in a small kitchen can be overwhelming, halting your productivity.

Storage: How will you store staples (sugar, flour, rice) and leftovers? Do you like decorative containers on the counter or prefer them stacked out of view in a pantry?

Occasional entertaining: Would you enjoy hosting a bridal or baby shower, or a girlfriend's brunch? Then think about punch bowls and cake plates. If you are more inclined to host a work-related or couples party, then consider serving dishes and tapas plates. Will you be throwing gameday parties? A large slow cooker, chip and dip set, and beverage coasters are ideal selections.

Will you deck the halls? Holiday entertainment opportunities are plentiful. Decide whether you'll have the opportunity to host and plan accordingly. Think roasting pan for Thanksgiving turkey or red place mats and napkins for Christmas.

The great outdoors: Will you picnic together or host backyard gatherings? Consider a blanket and picnic basket, beverage tub, cooler, or grill and bonfire accessories.

What do you like to eat? What culinary direction will you take in your kitchen—do you want a pizza stone, wok, fondue set? Steering toward healthier living? Maybe a juicer, immersion blender, or spiralizer would be the perfect motivational tool.

Coffee makers, juicers, etc. Prioritize small appliances according to frequency of use. Comparison shop online and then apply a realistic price point for each. Allot higher prices for quality on frequently used appliances.

The gift matrix: The rule of thumb is to scan, or register for approximately twice the number of items as invitations sent, (100 guests = 200 registry items). If you plan on registering at multiple stores, the total item count would include all of the shops. The calculation encompasses all gift-giving including: engagement parties, showers and the wedding itself. Surprised by that number? Consider how many of those items are smaller gadgets that a guest could likely bundle or add to the bow as added decoration. Think: mixing bowls embellished with a whisk tied in the bow.

What did you learn about each other from your in-store or online research?

Our Newlywed

KITCHEN

· ESSENTIALS CHECKLIST ·

Registry
THOUGHTS

....
....
....
....
....
....
....
....
....
....
....
....
....
....
....
....
_____

Ready or Knot

KITCHEN ESSENTIALS CHECKLIST

Whether you're starting from scratch to stock your kitchen or seeking a much-needed do-over, consider the comprehensive checklist of tools on the next few pages.

These are the basic tools you'll need to ensure culinary success, so the *Kitchen Essentials Checklist* is invaluable as you build your registry. Along with the checklist, I've included my own tips (*MyTip*) that are meant to guide you in what might work best in your kitchen. The checklist serves three purposes:

Confidence builder: Scrolling through endless web pages of culinary options or viewing multiple retail displays of cookware can be daunting. With your *Kitchen Essentials Checklist* in hand, you're armed with the information you need before you shop. Simply select the style, brand, or color of the item you desire. So breathe easy.

Efficiency guide: The checklist suggests how to get more mileage out of some tools as well as items that can be left off of your registry all together, leaving room for finer registry gifts that will last a lifetime.

Inventory taker: Here's your opportunity to replace, combine, or upgrade your current kitchen items. Do you have nesting bowls but two of them have chipped during several moves? Does he have well-worn pots and pans that need replacing? Investing the time to take inventory of what you both own, and what you still need, will pay big dividends when it comes time to shop your registry. Consider this process as practice in learning to work together and making compromises. ❧

Whether you're a foodie or a newbie in the kitchen, this list is ideal for basic food prep.

Use your registry as an opportunity to select lasting, quality essentials.

Cutting Boards

Wood, bamboo, teak, plastic, or glass? There are so many choices on the market, and probably a few more that didn't make the list. Here's the breakdown:

Wood, bamboo, and teak are easy on your knives, as they allow the knife to stick a little when the blade hits the board. This feature allows for better knife control and safety. Wood, bamboo and teak boards require more upkeep. They aren't dishwasher safe, so wash them by hand or disinfect them in the microwave for 30 to 60 seconds. Never leave them soaking in water. Over time, water separates wood, and they can crack and break, so occasionally treat them with mineral oil. Wood contains a natural bacterial resistant property that plastic doesn't.

Glass boards are easy to clean, but I've found that they become slippery after washing, break easily, and the sound of a knife on glass is just plain unnerving. Glass boards are not ideal for keeping knives sharp.

Plastic boards are inexpensive, dishwasher safe and less likely to dull your knives, but tend to stain and show wear more readily. New studies are showing that plastic boards may contain toxic chemicals that leach during use. Look for a board that does not contain BPA or other harmful chemicals.

MyTip: I prefer a board with anti-slip grips on the side. To avoid cross-contamination when cooking with meat, use more than one board. Dedicate a board for raw meat and another for everything else. A drip-well around the rim is a nice feature as it catches excess liquid. Less mess! Look for a board that's at least 15x20 inches so you'll have plenty of room to work. I Once your boards become overly scarred discontinue use in kitchen. For parties, a wood cutting board can also serve as a handsome charcuterie tray.

Start with the Basics

Knives

Knife block or individual knives? A block provides lots of cutlery options, is conveniently accessible on your counter top, stores knives safely, and many include steak knives. If you forgo the block and select knives individually, a chef's knife (used 80 percent of the time), serrated knife, paring knife, and boning knife will get you started. Store loose knives in a safety sleeve or on a magnetic strip. This will protect both you and your knives. Never place knives in the dishwasher, as high heat will dull the blades. For longer life, wash and dry by hand.

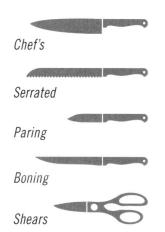

Chef's

Serrated

Paring

Boning

Shears

Cookware

This selection is sure to be the greatest challenge on your registry because of cost, frequency of use, and expected longevity. The essentials you will likely need are: stock pot with lid, Dutch oven, small and medium sauce pans with lids, large sauté pan with lid, and small sauté pan.

Keep these three points in mind as you research your cookware selection: **1.** Know your cooktop: is it a gas, electric coil, or ceramic-glass range? **2.** How's the pan's grip, feel, and weight? Is it comfortable? **3.** Do you prefer a glass lid for easy peeking?

Nonstick cookware has been around for many years and has gained popularity because of the ease of cooking and cleanup. Downside: They usually are not dishwasher safe, and you will want to be aware of studies on

Copper

Quality is key when selecting knives and cookware. Grow into them, not out of them.

Stainless Steel

Glass

COOKING ESSENTIALS

perfluorooctanoic acid (PFOA), a man-made chemical used in the process of making Teflon™ and similar nonstick chemicals. While the International Agency for Research on Cancer has classified PFOA as "possibly carcinogenic to humans," the American Cancer Society reports that studies show no known risks to humans from using Teflon-coated cookware.[1] Stainless steel, ceramic, glass, or cast iron may be safer alternatives.

Stainless Steel is durable, scratch-resistant, dishwasher safe, and completely recyclable. Because it is not a coated product it will never leach chemicals into your food and makes for easy scouring. Downside: Heat transfer is poor, unless the set offers a bonded core of aluminum or copper (also known as tri-ply), which helps in this area but adds to the price.

Cast Iron is an inexpensive and versatile workhorse that will last a lifetime. It has excellent heat distribution, which is great for simmering, browning, and searing. It also transfers well to the oven. Downside: It's heavy and not recommended for ceramic-glass cooktops or cooking acidic foods. When new, it requires "seasoning" (heating in the oven enabling it to become nonstick over use). Cleaning requires special care; use a scrubber sponge and coarse salt to remove debris. Drying well and lightly coating with oil after every use will prevent rusting.

Ceramic is the most versatile cookware as it is safe to use in the oven, microwave, refrigerator, and dishwasher. It's naturally nonstick and transfers nicely to the table, doubling as a serving dish. Downside: Ceramic is heavy and is prone to chipping and cracking.

Glass is inexpensive and retains heat longer than metal. Downside: It's heavy and can break if dropped. It can also be tough to clean and is not recommended for ceramic-glass cooktops.

Copper is one of the most beautiful of all your choices and widely used by chefs for its quick and even conduction of heat. If you plan to make the investment, choose a stainless steel-lined interior, as copper is highly reactive to acidic foods. Aluminum is also offered as an interior lining, however it doesn't wear as well. Downside: It comes with a hefty price tag and need for regular polishing. Copper is not dishwasher safe.

MyTip: *No one material will do it all. I suggest stainless steel for longevity and everyday use due to ease of cleanup, cast iron for searing meat, and a ceramic Dutch oven for soups and stews. Use a healthy oil when scrambling eggs and your stainless works like nonstick.*

Utensil Set

A basic set includes: **spoon, slotted spoon, slotted turner, ladle, and whisk**. Choose the material that works best with your cookware set: stainless steel, wood, or plastic. Wood, bamboo or plastic utensils won't scratch nonstick, or ceramic cookware. Any utensil style works with stainless steel. Downside: Plastic utensils can melt and leach toxins, wood utensils need care during cleaning and are not dishwasher safe.

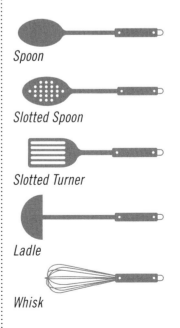

Spoon

Slotted Spoon

Slotted Turner

Ladle

Whisk

---

1. "Teflon and Perfluorooctanoic Acid (PFOA)," Amercian Cancer Society, https://www.cancer.org/cancer/cancer-causes/teflon-and-perfluorooctanoic-acid-pfoa.html.

Not all gifts come from a store. You might be lucky enough to be given a family heirloom like this vintage 1940s Pyrex Primary Colors Mixing Bowl Set.

BAKING ESSENTIALS

Baking Dish

A 9x13-inch pan is commonly used for everything from brownies to lasagna. This size is great if cooking for a crowd or taking a casserole or dessert to a party. Choose an 8x8-inch for smaller-portioned dishes. Metal versus glass? Metal: Better at conducting heat. This means it loses its heat quickly, too. Metal browns foods evenly and is great for roasting. Some metal baking dishes have nonstick surfaces for easy cleanup but can scratch if not cared for properly. Glass: Poor conductor of heat, which means it takes longer to heat up. But once it's hot, it holds heat longer. Think casseroles or dishes you'd like to keep warm and serve oven-to-table. Glass baking dishes are not recommended for broiling or direct high-heat cooking.

MyTip: Whether you choose glass or metal, opt for a boxed set. Wedding guests prefer to purchase gifts that are easy to wrap.

Cake Pans

Round cake pans, Bundt or tube pan—any of the three will make an impressive cake. If you choose round cake pans, be sure to register for two so you can make a layered cake. If you love to bake, choose all three.

Cookie Sheet Jelly Roll Pan

A cookie sheet is flat with one or two sides turned up for easy handling. The flat sides allow cookies to ease off the pan without disturbing their shape. Insulated cookie sheets prevent cookies from browning too quickly. A jelly roll pan, which is rimmed on all sides, is the more versatile choice. It's great for roasting vegetables and baking homemade pizza, Texas sheet cakes, and jelly roll cakes. It comes in two sizes ($15^1/_2$x$10^1/_2$-inch or 18x12-inch) with a one-inch lip. And you can use it to bake cookies, too.

MyTip: Unless cookies are your priority, go with a jelly roll pan for its versatility.

Measuring Cups

A **glass measuring cup** measures liquid in ounces while varied capacity **nesting cups** ($1/_4$ cup, $1/_3$ cup, $1/_2$ cup, 1 cup) are great for dry ingredients. Trust me, you'll be glad you have both.

Measuring Spoons

Every kitchen needs a set or two. No searching required if you choose a set linked together. This is a great place to show a little personality in your kitchen as they come in a wide variety of colors and styles.

Mixing Bowls

Plastic, ceramic, glass, or metal—you choose. A set of three usually covers your basic needs.

Muffin Tin

This tool for making muffins is also great for making single-serving appetizers or baked treats, too. Whether to buy six- or twelve-cup muffin tins depends on if you plan to bake cupcakes or treats for a crowd.

MyTip: Bake as much as possible at one time to save energy and time. I recommend registering for at least two of the six-cup tins or a single twelve-cup.

Pie Plate & Rolling Pin

Nothing says "home" like a pie in the oven. A pie plate is also useful in preparing savory dishes such as quiche, shepherd's pie, and pot pies. In a pinch, a pie plate can even serve as a small baking dish for casseroles, cornbread, cobbler, and bread pudding.

Don't be Surprised if you get pounded!

A "Pounding" is a special kind of shower meant to stock the newlyweds' pantry. The name comes from the gift of a pound of nonperishable food: dry pasta, lentils, beans, rice, salt, flour, sugar, brown sugar, oats, or other dry goods will work. Some pounding gifts will come in clever storage containers and contain more than the essentials, such as chocolate chips, nuts, and raisins.

These too!

Additional Essentials

Concerning the items in this category, the simpler, the better.

Can opener

Vegetable peeler

Silicone spatula

Ice cream scoop

Box grater

Garlic press

Meat thermometer

Kitchen tongs

Potato masher

Colander

You'll find these in plastic or stainless and in any color. In addition to rinsing potatoes and straining pasta, they can serve a dual-purpose as a salad spinner (with help from paper towels). In a pinch, you can use a stainless steel colander as a vegetable steamer. Some colanders come within cookware sets.

Dish Towels

Place function over form when making this selection.

1. Absorbency. They must simply do their job. Try terry cloth or waffle-weave towels in cotton for best results.

2. Durability. Look for quality towels that can withstand frequent washings or bleachings.

3. Style. Here's an opportunity to have a little fun as towels can set off the décor of your kitchen.

MyTip: The more print on a towel the less absorbent it becomes.

Oven Mitts

Choose a favorite color or print to match your kitchen décor. Beware of lightweight mitts; you need to protect that ring finger!

Storage Containers

Dry storage containers keep your staples fresh and organized. A stackable version saves space and fits nicely in a cabinet or on a pantry shelf, while canister sets are handy on the counter and look pretty. Don't forget about containers for storing leftovers in the refrigerator for a healthy lunch or in the freezer for an easy dinner.

Glass versus plastic: Glass storage containers are durable and resist stains. They come with airtight seals and are safe for dishwasher, freezer, microwave, and oven. Downside: Breakable.

Plastic storage containers are inexpensive, stackable, and come with tight seals for preserving cold foods. Downside: Although some sets are labeled BPA Free, do your homework before you buy. Where possible, check the bottom of the container for the coded triangle number symbol. The numbers will range from 1 to 7, indicating the type of plastic. The safest choices for your health are 2, 4, and 5.

Tongs

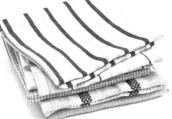

Dish Towels

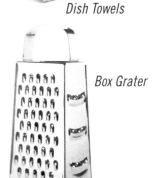

Box Grater

Vegetable Peeler

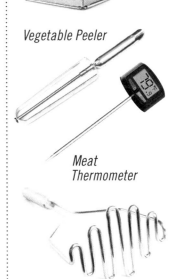

Meat Thermometer

Potato Masher

Kitchen Essentials

KITCHEN ESSENTIALS CHECKLIST

Baking Items

- ☐ Baking dishes
- ☐ Cake pans
- ☐ Measuring cups
- ☐ Measuring spoons
- ☐ Muffin tins
- ☐ Oven mitts
- ☐ Pie plate
- ☐ Rolling pin
- ☐ Round cake pan
- ☐ Silicone spatulas

Storage Containers

- ☐ Countertop
- ☐ Pantry
- ☐ Refrigerator/Freezer

Cookware Sets

- ☐ Cast iron skillet
- ☐ Dutch oven
- ☐ Stock pot with lid
- ☐ Small sauce pan with lid
- ☐ Medium sauce pan with lid
- ☐ Large sauté pan with lid
- ☐ Small sauté pan

Cutlery

- ☐ Boning
- ☐ Chef's
- ☐ Paring
- ☐ Serrated
- ☐ Shears

Cutting Boards

- ☐ Wood
- ☐ Plastic
- ☐ Other

Mixing Bowls

- ☐ Nesting set of 3

Tools & Utensils

- ☐ Box grater
- ☐ Can opener
- ☐ Colander
- ☐ Cooking thermometer
- ☐ Dish towels
- ☐ Ice cream scoop
- ☐ Kitchen tongs
- ☐ Ladle
- ☐ Potato masher
- ☐ Silicon spatula
- ☐ Slotted spoon
- ☐ Slotted turner
- ☐ Serving spoon
- ☐ Vegetable peeler
- ☐ Whisk

Small Appliances

- ☐ Blender
- ☐ Coffee maker
- ☐ Slow cooker
- ☐ Griddle
- ☐ Hand mixer
- ☐ Tea kettle
- ☐ Toaster/Toaster oven

ADDITIONAL ITEMS

- ☐
- ☐
- ☐
- ☐
- ☐
- ☐
- ☐
- ☐
- ☐
- ☐
- ☐
- ☐
- ☐
- ☐
- ☐
- ☐
- ☐
- ☐
- ☐

PRINT A CHECKLIST AT

OurNewlywedKitchen.com

FINE DINNERWARE

LAURA SCHUPP

Think long-term when selecting a dinnerware pattern. Contemporary styles change, but simple, classic elegance never goes out of style.

My Traditional Take

When I became newly engaged the trend was to register for fine dinnerware, crystal, and flatware, but not much else. I was even given a "china shower" hosted by my aunt. My relatives and well-meaning sales clerks suggested that if I didn't receive those niceties now, I would never purchase them after the wedding. They were too expensive and not an essential that fit our humble budget.

Fine dinnerware was looked upon as something to be treasured and eventually handed down—a keepsake. It was a right of passage for a young woman entering marriage. There may have been some status attached to the choices as well.

Looking back, the women in my circle were in such a hurry to grow up and appear established. Apparently, we thought that owning branded dishes by Lenox, Mikasa, Wedgewood, and Waterford would get us there.

As I recall, the broad array of place settings were themed in varied color palettes set over white or bone, with silver or gold rims, but maybe that was just where my tastes landed at the time. I was infatuated with the colors of the decade: peach and teal, mauve and Wedgewood blue. I don't recall seeking or receiving much advice concerning my selection. My mistake. Today, I feel I erred in my selection—not by choosing to register for fine dinnerware, nor in the number of place settings I chose, but in the pattern itself.

Today, I feel I erred in my selection.

While I love the style of my bone china: the slender, timeless mold of the plates; the delicate form of the cups; and the elegant size of the serving platters and bowls; I almost never use them. My error was in siding with the popular colors of the time—subtle scrolls of peach and teal on a bone backdrop. I haven't used them as much as their expensive price tag warranted. And because those colors have cycled out of style, I hesitated to pass them down to my daughter. I am continually trying to find ways to update them, but I fear they will forever be branded by the 80s.

If I had the chance to register again, I would still choose eight place settings but in a timeless, understated pattern with matching crystal and flatware. I would still select fine dinnerware, because I love setting an elegant table. And again, I would seek to mark our wedded union with this unforgettable heirloom, dreaming of the daughter who would someday receive my precious horde. Yet, the place setting I most often use is from the white, silver-rimmed, boxed set of fine china my very practical mother-in-law, Emma, generously gave us.

She cleverly bought three sets, since buying in sets offers a greater value, so whether the family individually or collectively entertained, we were able to borrow from each other and use 24 place settings. I use these pieces most often because I'm not worried about chipping them since we have a vast collection, they are easy to replace, and they match any holiday or special occasion as the style is timeless. My daughter, under my advice, opted for her own set of fine dinnerware. Yet she hosts a different opinion on the topic.

CASUAL DINNERWARE

ELISE SCHUPP MORRIS

Elise Chimes In

I've noticed that registering for fine dinnerware is not common among my peers. Maybe it's because it seems like an outdated idea, or this generation of bride doesn't think they'll ever use it.

When it came time for me and my fiancé to start our registry, I selected a place setting of Bone china I liked without hesitation. Seeing my mom and grandmother have multiple sets themselves, many of which had been passed down from my great grandmothers, I just followed suit. But after a few weeks of making decisions about this appliance or that glass and how the colors and styles were relating to one another, I began to doubt my selections. I wondered how I would store all of these fine pieces, or if it was realistic to move them with us since our future included military relocations. Would I use them? I debated even keeping them on my registry.

For the first three years of our marriage the five place settings of fine dinnerware I received (we registered for eight) remained in their original packaging. In all that time we hadn't found a reason to unwrap and use them. It seemed like a waste to remove them from their bubble wrap when I knew I'd be packing them up again in a few months as we made a trek halfway across the country. To be frank, I wasn't sure I wanted to keep them. I could address this "fine dining" situation by simply dressing up the table while using my basic white casual dinnerware and adding beautiful accent plates, cloth napkins and napkin rings, chargers, candlesticks, and water goblets. There were (and always are) more ways to accomplish the task.

As silly as it may seem, what it took for me to finally decide to keep the fine dinnerware place settings was a refurbished antique hutch. I was so glad to have dishes actually worth displaying in my newly purchased piece. I don't use them often, but I know special occasions will arise, and I'll feel more than relieved that I can set a beautiful table with ease. And, when you think about it, do you even need a reason to have a romantic, candlelit dinner for two?

How to Select Your Dinnerware

$ Earthenware is lower in cost if you aren't ready to invest in china yet, but it chips easily. These dishes are offered in many colors and are microwave and dishwasher safe, making them ideal for everyday use.

$$ Stoneware is chip resistant and more durable because it's fired at higher temperatures. Its off-white color comes from the grey or brown clay used during production and a glaze application. Stoneware is a great choice for everyday use, especially if chipping will bother you. It is also microwave and dishwasher safe.

$$$ Porcelain is made with white clay, which gives it a pure white look. It's simple, elegant, and timeless, offering a good choice if you're looking for a versatile set for both everyday and fine dining. Porcelain is most often purchased for commercial use.

$$$$ Bone china is made of a mixture of refined clay and bone ash making it the strongest and most expensive dinnerware. It isn't recommended for the microwave or dishwasher, making it impractical for everyday use but ideal for fine dining. If you choose it, use it and don't worry about chipping.

Candlesticks, Vases, & Napkins with Rings

TRENDING

Check out the top-picks from online registries everywhere for great new style trends.

Classic-Pattern Fine Dinnerware

You'll want to make a selection that will last a lifetime, so choose a pattern that will reflect your style and also stand the test of time. Stick with simple, elegant patterns and colors (think crisp white with a metallic rim or simple detail). They will remain beautiful for decades, even as trends change.

All-White Casual Dinnerware

Brides today are finding that all-white dinnerware is a must-have on their wedding registries. Classic, fresh, and versatile, white dinnerware is great year round. It's easily dressed up for holidays and special occasions, yet simple enough for everyday use. With so many different options on the market, mixing it up is easy. Play with all-white designs and textures to add interest to your table, or select colorful fun accent plates and seasonal pieces to create a festive table year-round. Be sure to choose something that's durable and easy to replace. Whether you're a tablescape expert or new at finding your way around a kitchen, you won't be disappointed with this trend.

Fun Accent Plates

And speaking of adding variety, accent plates are sure to punch up the interest on any table. Whatever your style may be, you can find colorful, seasonal, or just plain quirky side plates to spice up your simple dinnerware. Peacocks, and foxes, and flowers, oh my!

MyTip: *Instead of an entire set of holiday dinnerware, opt for seasonal accent plates to enhance your holiday table. It'll make a big impact, (as a little holiday goes a long way), with fewer dishes to store.*

Don't Forget the Tabletop

Tablecloths, placemats, runners, chargers, cloth napkins, and napkin rings all add to the tablescape vibe you'll create. When making your selections, think how each piece will work together. The goal is to mix and match so you can create different looks for all occasions. Vases and candlesticks are perfect presentation pieces for mood and color on your table.

MyTip: *Think minimal. Let your occasional pieces (bowls, trays, vases) become multi-functional. A simple pitcher serves as a beverage dispenser, a piece of art, or a container for flowers.*

Glassware & Flatware

Casual Glasses

Juice and Tumbler: Typically paired with casual dinnerware, the options are endless. Look for a style that will complement your dinnerware selection. My rule of thumb: pick two sizes (Juice Glass, approx. 11 ounces, Cold Beverage Tumbler, approx. 16 ounces). A product that's affordable and always in-stock can be easily replaced if broken. Make sure you like the feel and weight of the glass in your hand.

MyTip: This is not the time to shop online. Ask your registry consultant (available at most fine registry departments) to set a mock table of your pattern choice(s) of dinnerware, glassware, and flatware selections. Mix and match all pieces until you achieve that "I love it!" moment. Be sure to include placemats, chargers, napkins, and rings to complete the look you are going for.

Glass Versus Crystal: Glass is great for everyday use, is dishwasher safe, and affordable to replace. Crystal, also called mineral glass, is delicate but strong. Lead gives it a light-refracting quality—the sparkle effect. The mineral composition allows it to be spun thin at the rim, which adds enjoyment to each sip. It is not dishwasher safe and comes with a higher price tag. If you have the storage space, this high-end option is sure to look dazzling alongside your fine dinnerware.

Flatware

Sterling Silver, Silverplate, & Stainless Steel: Sterling silver and silver plate are durable, but require hand washing, drying, and polishing. When selecting fine flatware, look for the chrome-to-nickel ratio stamp (18/8 good or 18/10 better). The first number denotes strength, the second, luster. Stainless steel is often used with casual dinnerware because it's dishwasher safe. Look for a style that complements your chosen dinnerware set(s) and feels good in your hand.

Hostess Serveware includes: tablespoon, slotted tablespoon, casserole spoon, cold meat fork, serving knife, gravy ladle, cake/pie server, and smaller items such as butter knives and sugar spoons.

MyTip: Boxed sets of flatware usually come in sets of eight or twelve place settings, with five pieces in each setting, and they generally include a hostess set. For added value, look for sets that include matching steak knives.

Dinnerware Checklist

Your Registry Decision

By now, you've read the suggested comments on dinnerware and are ready to make a decision. On this page, I've listed the essentials you'll need whether you're choosing fine, casual, or both. If you choose casual and plan to forgo fine dinnerware, it's wise to lean toward a simple pattern, higher quality, and more place settings. The standard rule of thumb is at least eight, and no more than twelve. If selecting both, let them complement each other in style, and allow one to out dress the other.

I've also added a helpful *QuickStart Questionnaire* to assist you in your decision-making. Depending on your answers, you'll be led through the basic pieces for dinnerware, glassware, flatware, and serveware. Be sure to use this *QuickStart* as a pre-shop to your registry. It's easy and comprehensive.

Your choices will become clearer as you narrow your options in person with a registry consultant, building your place setting from the placemat up. I know you'll make wonderful selections that reflect your personality and lifestyle.

Like your marriage, your dinnerware will last a lifetime. Choose wisely, and enjoy the experience.

What's your dinnerware decision?

- [ ] **Fine dinnerware**
- [ ] **Casual dinnerware**
- [ ] **Both. We like to keep our options open.**
- [ ] **Skipping this selection. We won't require either option.**

Choose a pattern!

- [ ] **White, or off-white rimmed in gold or silver**
- [ ] **Oriental or exotic**
- [ ] **Geometric, to match the clean lines of our décor**
- [ ] **Floral and feminine**
- [ ] **Mix and match—to keep things laid-back**

How many settings?

- [ ] **8 or fewer—We're into intimate gatherings.**
- [ ] **10 feels about right.**
- [ ] **12—We do things big.**

Flatware style?

- [ ] **Stainless steel—durable**
- [ ] **Plated silver—striking but not pretentious**
- [ ] **Sterling silver—heirloom quality**

Casual Dinnerware

Essentials Dinnerware (one per setting)

- [ ] Dinner Plate
- [ ] Salad/Dessert Plate
- [ ] Soup/Cereal Bowl
- [ ] Mug

Also Consider

- [ ] Platter
- [ ] Serving Bowl (2)

Essentials Glassware (one per setting)

- [ ] Cold Beverage Glass
- [ ] Juice Glass

Essentials Flatware (one per setting)

- [ ] Dinner Knife
- [ ] Salad Fork
- [ ] Steak Knife (optional)
- [ ] Soupspoon
- [ ] Dinner Fork
- [ ] Teaspoon

Hostess Serveware

- [ ] Tablespoon (2)
- [ ] Pierced Table Spoon

Fine Dinnerware

Essentials (one per setting)

- [ ] Dinner Plate
- [ ] Cup with Saucer
- [ ] Salad/Dessert Plate
- [ ] Bread Plate
- [ ] Soup Bowl
- [ ] Charger (optional)

Additional Fine Dinnerware Pieces

- [ ] Large Platter
- [ ] Salt & Pepper
- [ ] Small Platter
- [ ] Cream Pitcher
- [ ] Large Serving Bowl
- [ ] Sugar Bowl
- [ ] Small Vegetable Bowl (2)
- [ ] Gravy Boat

Essentials Glassware

- [ ] Water Goblet

Essentials Flatware (one per setting)

- [ ] Dinner Knife
- [ ] Teaspoon
- [ ] Dinner Fork
- [ ] Butter Knife (optional)
- [ ] Salad Fork
- [ ] Cake Fork (optional)
- [ ] Salad Knife (optional)
- [ ] Dessert Spoon (optional)
- [ ] Soupspoon

Hostess Serveware

- [ ] Tablespoon (3)
- [ ] Gravy Ladle
- [ ] Slotted Table Spoon (2)
- [ ] Pie/Cake Server
- [ ] Cold Meat Fork
- [ ] Casserole Spoon
- [ ] Serving Knife

Our Newlywed
KITCHEN

Your Secret Weapon

Kitchen Experiences You'll Tackle Together

Gone are the days of gender separateness in the kitchen—that's why the role your fiancé will play couldn't be placed in the back of the book as an afterthought. He'll share in everything from selecting what *goes in* your kitchen as you complete your registry, to what's *served up* while applying the 21-Dinner Rotation system I'll introduce later. As a team, you'll work together, not only in the kitchen—the heart of the home—but also in the spiritual, financial, relational, and wellness aspects of life. And the best thing is, he's ready for it.

Sure, your guy might not be a top chef, but he is savvy enough to know he's needed at all levels of kitchen duty and beyond. Start with the grill, an area men tend to enjoy. But his involvement goes deeper than that. You can share duties when it comes to the planning, shopping, prepping, cooking, and cleaning in the kitchen. Some of these tasks you'll wish to handle yourself, while sharing other duties that fit him best. I personally enjoy being alone as I plan the menu and shop, but I think cooking and cleanup are more enjoyable when they are shared. I encourage you to consider each other's strengths and schedules, and then decide who will be responsible for the various tasks.

I'm calling your fiancé a "Secret Weapon," because I don't want you to underestimate his value in the kitchen and as operating as teammates. While a man's involvement in the kitchen has increased, it's still not on par with a woman's. A recent research survey showed that 43 percent of men did food preparation and cleanup activities versus 70 percent of women.[2] So as you talk about who does what, I'd like to share the benefits of working together in this space. No matter whose job or turn it is, it's certainly more rewarding if the tasks are done together. And as you join forces, your marriage will benefit.

2. American Time Use Survey, Charts by Topic: Household Activities, Bureau of Labor Statistics, https://www.bls.gov/TUS/CHARTS/HOUSEHOLD.HTM

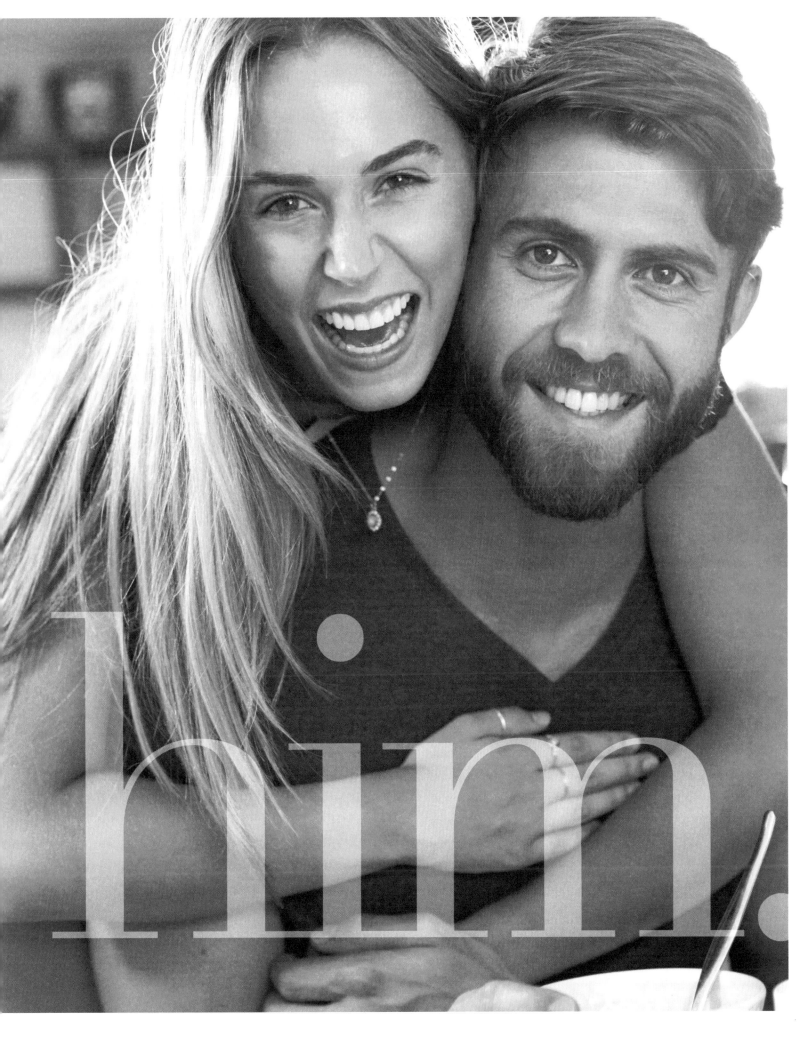

him.

Build Connection

The dinnertime prep sets the stage for communication between the two of you, which is key to a healthy marriage. Healthy, face-to-face communication is a learned skill that calls for practice. And you can practice daily as you connect during this easy, task-oriented routine. As more difficult topics come up for discussion, you will have already established a strong foundation through this nightly face-time.

Support Health

Healthy living takes discipline, but you have each other for support and accountability. This kind of reinforcement proves valuable in several areas. Avoid the pre-dinner snacking calories by scheduling the evening meal. You can encourage each other to ignore those pizza cravings when fresh fish is waiting in the fridge. Together, decide which after-dinner sweet temptations are allowed in the house. You also can pack leftovers for lunch the next day, so you both stay on track.

Find Strengths

Seek out and appreciate each other's strengths. Sharing kitchen duties doesn't mean you'll take on identical roles. As a matter of fact, it means the opposite. Through these routine tasks, you'll discover each other's skill set. If your guy has a talent for cooking, assist him with the food prep. If he's better at finding the best grocery deals, hand him the list. This sets the foundation for finding strengths and compatibility in other areas of life.

Count Pennies

Grab hold of your budget by choosing to eat at home most nights and by saving the leftovers for lunches. Make it fun through friendly competition. Who can plan the most frugal, tasty, or adventurous meal? Take turns and keep score! I hold the record in our marriage for planning the most frugal dinner date night. I found a boxed spaghetti dinner on clearance for a dollar (this was before we decided to get healthy) and took him to dollar night at the movies, forgoing the popcorn and soda.

Another benefit to sharing the responsibility of the grocery budget and shopping is a mutual understanding and agreement of why meatless or low-cost meals show up on the menu far more often than steak.

Make Memories

Prepping dinner together may seem mundane, but it's really all in how you spin it. Make the most of your time together. Learn to find comfort, entertainment, peace, nourishment, and fun as you jointly tackle the tasks at hand. Get comfortable, play music, dance, brew some Matcha green tea, or sip on your favorite beverage. What will you learn about each other tonight? What memories will you make?

Use this *QuickStart* as a guide to find his strengths. If he isn't already onboard, challenge him to speak into this topic, since this will lead to shared kitchen responsibilities.

He enjoys the kitchen . . .

☐ and is willing to share the duties.

☐ and wants to take over.

☐ like a poke in the eye with a sharp stick.

Because of his cooking experience, he . . .

☐ thinks Ramen noodles are a staple.

☐ knows his way around a sauce pan.

☐ finds milk & cereal a challenge.

He'd be most comfortable at . . .

☐ the grill.

☐ the cooktop.

☐ the sink.

If he were to cook, he'd make . . .

1.

2.

3.

Swapping kitchen duties will keep things fresh and exciting. Let your new husband take the helm, giving him room to surprise you with his culinary skills.

SECRET WEAPON *Points of Interest*

You'll both benefit from the fruits of his labor, so help him find an area of expertise. When the pressure is on, you'll be able to divide and conquer.

Grocery shopping: With budget in mind and a detailed list in-hand, your Secret Weapon (SW) can be released to the aisles and come home with the goods. The shop is an area that requires great discernment and should not be left to impulse purchases, e.g., "I always wanted to sample sardines in mustard sauce." Don't laugh, it happens. On the other hand, you may be getting hitched to a wizard in the kitchen, someone who knows a good cut of meat. If this is your SW, he'll be invaluable as you both plan your meals and shop.

Clean up: It's as easy as "You load the dishwasher, while I get dessert ready." Sounds pretty fair to me, and it's worked for many years. Fact is, a shared after-dinner routine will allow for more time to spend together at the end of the day. Later on in life, it will teach the little ones about a loving marriage as they watch you work in tandem.

Food specialties: Every man needs something that only he makes. Through the ages, men have claimed barbecues, gumbos, and game-day cuisine as their domain. My secret weapon, Thom, upon ordering an amazing Caesar salad at a world-renowned restaurant in Tampa, Florida, came to the conclusion that he would duplicate it for home consumption. He established a strong rapport with the waiter and watched closely as the salad was prepared tableside. To this day, Thom is known for two dishes that he takes great pride in making: Oysters Apalachicola and that borrowed Caesar salad recipe. You'll find that most signature dishes come when your betrothed finds something that fits his cravings, which prompts a desire to have it as often as possible.

The grill: Let him make his mark in the outdoor kitchen. The grill is a great place to test his culinary abilities. But it isn't just for steak anymore, as everything from fish, veggies, tortillas, and pizza can wind up there. His mission is to always have the propane tank full and the grill grates clean. Remember to add grilling utensils and a meat thermometer to your registry!

Mixations: Today's farm-to-table food explosion is spilling over to the beverage bar and beyond with the resurrection of classic brews such as lavender lemonade and watermelon mint tea, and the invention of highly sophisticated blendables. The fresher the ingredients the better. The tools he'll need for the job need not be expensive, but a great blender makes the process more enjoyable and produces better outcomes for smoothies, shakes, and other frozen concoctions. For recipes go to *OurNewlywedKitchen.com.*

The knife master: The registry introduces him to what could become one of his areas of expertise—chopping and cutting. When choosing the cutlery for your kitchen, put him in charge. (See Knives in the *Kitchen Essentials* chapter.) Once he's taken ownership of the sharp stuff, he'll be only too happy to debone a chicken or chop the broccoli.

The bond you build around your table and *in your kitchen* will have a lifelong affect on your marriage.

A PRAYER FOR
Togetherness

....

....

....

....

....

....

....

....

....

....

....

....

....

MARK 10: 8-9 ESV

"And the two shall become one flesh. So they are no longer two but one flesh.
What therefore God has joined together, let not man separate."

Pause, & take a Deep Breath

THAT'S ENOUGH FOR NOW.
GO FOCUS ON YOUR DRESS.

———◆◆◆———

PICK UP FROM HERE AFTER YOUR NUPTIALS.

Our Newlywed
KITCHEN
· SOMETHING BORROWED ·

Something old, Something new, Something BORROWED, Something blue and a sixpence IN HER SHOE.

Something BORROWED

This Old English rhyme is meant as a good luck charm for the newlywed couple.
"Something borrowed" symbolizes borrowed happiness. Whose marriage or family do you admire?
Who has passed on happy traditions to you? In my youth, many women mentored me
through their God-given gifts and talents. And now I feel my calling is to pass on these strengths
to my daughter, future daughters-in-law, and brides-to-be everywhere.
After all, in order to borrow, someone else must be willing to share!

PAPA

I come from a long line of women who loved to cook, but this story actually begins
with my paternal grandfather, Alonzo Jerome. A descendant of the French Huguenots
originally from South Carolina, "Papa," as we affectionately called him, decided to
move to St. Petersburg, Florida, indirectly changing our name and family lineage along
the way.

Upon arriving in St. Pete, Papa and his brother, Jim, worked for an ice company
that inadvertently dispensed paychecks with the incorrect spelling of their last name,
Furqueron. Rather than make waves, they assumed the new version, which simply
replaced the first "u" with an "e," resulting in Ferqueron. I love this story, in part
because it represents a simpler time, and because it reveals my grandfather as the
easygoing, calm-natured man he was.

The story also illustrates the ease with which all of us can impact and change our
family history forever. Good or bad, we all have within us the ability to positively
redesign our family tree. Quite frankly, we can't choose the family we are born into,
but we can choose to craft the family we would like to have. As the bride, you have an
opportunity to prepare for your future family today.

Grace

NANA

Papa's wife, my paternal grandmother, Grace Aline, was tall, slender, and always donned an apron. She had a bashful laugh that said she could tolerate a little playful ribbing. We all called her Nana—even the adults. I don't know a lot about her upbringing except that she was from Ft. Myers, Florida, and her father had a "fiery" disposition. Luckily she didn't inherit it. She often spoke of fond memories of her mother baking homemade cinnamon rolls and leaving them on an open windowsill to cool just in time for school to let out. She followed the scent home and was the envy of the neighborhood. What I do remember most about Nana? That woman could cook!

That woman could cook!

My personal favorite were her angel biscuits, always plentiful, light and fluffy, and dripping with butter. To this day my husband says he's never eaten a Reuben sandwich to rival one of Nana's. But her biggest crowd pleaser—the signature item that accompanied her wherever she was invited—was her chocolate chip cookies. They were lovingly transported in a large celery-colored Tupperware bowl bearing a worn paper label on the lid with her faded name, "Grace Ferqueron." This one memory spoke volumes about her character. Influenced by the Great Depression as most of her generation was, she was somewhat frugal and a good steward of her possessions. But her food, the fruit of her labor, was the gift she freely gave.

She was kind-hearted and generous, and she paid great attention to the details. Her special trait was keeping track of everyone's food preferences. I don't know how she kept it all straight in a family our size, but I can still remember hearing her exclaim as the meal was being served, "Laura doesn't like that!"

Looking back, I realize that Nana always made me feel as if I belonged. What stands out most is how Nana's nurturing made me feel connected and special. She took a great interest in my likes and dislikes, and that meant I mattered.

Nana and Papa's only daughter, my aunt, was adoringly called Ouie, pronounced (o–'e–). She was adorned with this name because my father, Alonzo Jerome, Jr., couldn't pronounce her given name of Dolores. I'm guessing no one ever corrected him, since he was eight years her junior and the baby of the family. How you phonetically bridge the two names never made any sense to me, but I chose to shrug it off and retain this little nugget of our family history.

Ouie marked her place in our family with her distinctly recognizable laugh. The full and robust sound was mimicked by many in jest but never matched. As a second grade teacher, she had a special gift of caring for children. Even in a crowded room, she took time to look into the eyes of the youngest children and greet them, giving them connection and worth in the days when "children were seen and not heard" was the popular sentiment. But the real thing you need to know about Ouie, and the quality from which we all benefited is this: she was the glue of the family.

She was the glue of the family.

I don't know where it all started, but it was evident to me from an early age that we gathered because Ouie called us together. Both her laugh and her home were warm and inviting. In her kitchen was a long, U-shaped counter that served as a buffet for large celebratory spreads. On those Sundays after church, the family room became a rowdy and boisterous den for the men, filled with the clamor of afternoon football. The women usually unwound after the midday meal (and the subsequent cleaning of the dishes) around the dining room table. The rest of the afternoon they would share recipes and swap interesting tidbits and family news. To avoid the chore, we children would scatter to build forts and three-story dollhouses with Ouie's vast collection of Encyclopedia Britannica in the Florida room, an all-seasoned screened enclosure with terrazzo floors and brightly colored palm fabrics.

I took those casual, contented family gatherings after church for granted back then. Even after I married and moved away, thinking of home meant gathering at Ouie's and belonging to something bigger. When she unexpectedly passed away, I felt something stir deep inside me. Who would carry on her traditions to the next generation?

I had always been in awe of the way Ouie gathered folks together with such ease, grace, and warmth. As far back as I can remember, I shared a deep connection with her, akin to that moment when you suddenly realize what you want to be when you grow up. I wanted to grow up to be like her. I wanted to know for certain that I could raise a family who felt loved and nurtured, a family who would long to return home. Mostly, in her absence, I desired our family gatherings to carry on with the unity and bonds she'd built. While no one could fill her shoes, I felt I needed to honor her memory and at least try to become our family gatherer.

BETTY JEAN & KATHRYN

Betty Jean and Kathryn are sisters, first cousins to Ouie, and all best friends since birth. Their mother, Kitty, was Nana's closest sister out of five siblings. I don't remember much about Kitty, but I'm told the lot of them could sit around all afternoon discussing recipes as if it were good gossip. Betty Jean, the older of the two, was the master planner of parties and events. She was the first woman I knew who would venture into weddings and catering and other fancy affairs. I experienced her exquisite taste and etiquette as she helped me plan my wedding.

Her husband, Moe, built her a beautiful home in the deep, thick pines and palmettos of Dunedin, Florida. Complete with five bedrooms, it was big enough for her brood of large boys, my rough and tumble cousins. The kitchen hosted a long counter made of one solid piece of natural cypress. It was the backdrop for truly elegant party buffets and holiday spreads.

Kathryn, on the other hand, liked to play the rebel and acted as though she really didn't understand what all the fuss was about. I think that happens when two sisters are as close in age as they are. Nonetheless, we had Easter celebrations at Kathryn's because she lived steps from a beach. I think she might have chosen that holiday to host because she could emphasize that casual dining with paper plates and plastic tablecloths had its place. She brought a sense of balance to all the fuss and formality. To this day, her bunny cake with licorice whiskers and green-dyed coconut grass rivals anything I've seen on Pinterest.

My mother, Diane, married into all this cooking, planning, and hosting. It wasn't her natural area of expertise, since she preferred practicing her piano and reading thick novels, but she had an easy, adaptable spirit, and aimed to please my father. A complete novice in the kitchen before marriage, as the story goes, she came running into the living room screaming, "The water is burning!"

Well, we all have a place to start. Her unique spin on what my Nana eventually taught her was the budget angle. We grew up very humbly in my early years (my father often exclaiming he could stand on a nickel and tell if it was heads or tails), so my mom needed to stretch her grocery dollars. Mom was a wise steward.

Mom was a wise steward.

After looking at the ads and computing her coupons, she often knew her final grocery tally to the penny before arriving at the store. She had to, as credit cards weren't the norm, and we certainly didn't have one.

One grocery shopping trip in particular stands out. We frequented Webb's City every two weeks after Dad received his paycheck, because it was the least expensive store in town. Bear in mind, Webb's City was known as *The World's Most Unusual Drugstore*. Unlike the local A&P or Winn Dixie, Webb's City was a four- story department store with outbuildings that featured a mermaid show, live animal arcade, barber shop, ice cream parlor, furniture store, plant nursery, and even a multi-bay gas station.

At nine years of age, and the oldest of three, I had several daunting responsibilities while shopping there. First, I had to keep my little brothers from wandering off in this enormous, magical building. Second, and more critical, was the task of choosing ten Kool-Aid packets from the vast variety of fruity flavors (no nine-year-old needs that kind of pressure). For far too long I stood there choosing a flavor, replacing it, and then choosing another until I eventually placed all ten in our cart. Finally, with arms stretched wide, I became the skinny link between our two-cart train, mother pushing while I safely navigated us through the crowded aisles. On that day, when we arrived at the checkout, the bill ran over.

On that day, when we arrived at the checkout, the bill ran over.

Mom was short on cash, embarrassed, yet somehow bold. She knew what she had to do. She looked at me with a disappointed expression, and then gave me the nod. I knew I would have to forfeit the meticulously selected Kool-Aid and even the potato chips. Though I was sad to see my mom embarrassed that day, I didn't mind giving up our treats. I was proud of her. She was living within her means and teaching us to do the same. She was taking care of us and doing the very best she could with what God provided. I gleaned quite a bit from those grocery shopping expeditions—respect for my mother and maybe a keener understanding of the sacrifices she was making for us.

I was too young to realize then, but they modeled, shaped, and anchored me to an understanding of family, food, nurturing, and belonging.

These women were my world.

They defined our clan through their unique skills and gifts. They embraced me with their love, goodness, and knowledge, and in turn I absorbed it like a sponge. I do miss those early years of gathering together, but what I am left with are the lessons I borrowed from each of them:

Nana's love of cooking,

Ouie's sense of gathering,

Betty Jean's social elegance,

Kathryn's practicality,

and Mom's keen eye on the budget.

These women anchored me to an understanding of family, food, nurturing, and belonging. Now it's your turn to consider the lessons you have "borrowed" from your loved ones.

I feel my calling is to pass on these strengths to my daughter, future daughters-in-law, and brides-to-be everywhere. After all, in order to borrow, someone else must be willing to share.

MY STORY OF Belonging

Who has made a profound impact on your life? Perhaps you were blessed enough to have a community of support. Use these pages to remember those very special someones.

....
....
....
....
....
....
....
....
....
....
....
....
....
....

Our Newlywed

KITCHEN

RECIPE COLLECTION

Cheese Cakes –

mix 1/2 Cup Sugar
     1/2 tsp Almond Extract
     1 EGG
     8oz Cream Cheese

Sprinkle bottom of Cup
Cake holders. w/ graham
Cracker Crumbs.
Pour Cream Cheese into
12 Cup Cakes.
Bake at 375
about 12 Min

SOMETHING OLD

There is something very intimate and special about a recipe collection.

I tend to hold mine dear like others would a photo album of their children—placed in the same category of things you would protect from a fire or gather if you had to leave in a hurry.

To some, recipes are mere ingredients on a page—a pathway to nourishment—but to me they conjure up familiar stories of past gatherings and friendships, snapshots of the roads I've traveled, and memories of the people I've met.

I took a break and spent some time reorganizing my recipes for the season. There was a crispness in the fall air that had me craving pumpkin latte and apple cake, so I went searching for a sweet and simple dessert to make with the ingredients I had on hand. I was secretly looking for a good reason to fire up the oven. What I uncovered was a recipe from an old friend that dates back nearly 25 years.

Sometimes God wraps gifts in the shape of a person.

We'd just built a home in the same area where I grew up in St. Petersburg, Florida, about a mile from the beach. Moving day marked our daughter's 11-month birthday, and I had just left my job to begin my new journey as a stay-at-home mom. I'd imagined having all sorts of neighborhood friends to converse with during the day, now that I had control of my time. Instead, I found myself at a different stage in life from the women nearby, since they weren't yet married with children. Suffice it to say, I was rather lonely in my new role. A few years passed, so I started traveling to the other side of town to meet up with other moms. After I had my son, Taylor, I finally ventured out to a nearby playgroup called Hug-a-Baby, in search of friends and sanity. It was there I met Jackie. She was from New York and had two daughters very close in age to my children. They had just moved in down the street. Our children quickly became playmates, and I had a new companion with a pool.

Jackie was quick and consistent with her invitations to come over. I found myself rushing around in the mornings to complete my household tasks so we could begin the fun. Her house was casual and lively, since new Hug-a-Baby friends always seemed to be dropping by with their children. She believed in an open door policy, and many times we would just bring over whatever groceries we had on hand and pull lunch together, talking, sipping iced tea, and letting the kids swim until afternoon. She had great ideas too, and we found ourselves on bike rides, transporting our kids and picnic lunches to the nearby parks on the water. I found I loved getting out during the day, and then taking my exhausted, sun-kissed babies home to rest in the afternoon while I prepared dinner.

After five years in our neighborhood, my husband and I prayed over the decision to move our family to Tennessee. Jackie never flinched when I told her the news, even though I knew she would be feeling the void. She simply asked if I had thoroughly thought it through, because she knew firsthand the hardship of taking babies away from grandparents. She was looking for a glimmer of hope … a chance we'd reconsider and stay.

The recipe is purely delightful.

Following the move, we visited Jackie and family every year when returning to Florida to see the grandparents, but new siblings had been added to the mix, and the dynamics just weren't the same. The Christmas cards came year after year, but the phone calls were few. Drifting apart was no one's fault; we each understood that family responsibilities came first. And then one afternoon I received a phone call from a mutual friend and member of our long ago playgroup. Jackie had passed away unexpectedly. It was a shock to everyone because she was still so young, had children to raise, dreams of her own to pursue, and a husband with whom she'd planned to share them.

As I flipped through the well-worn, stained pages of my first recipe collection on that fall day not long ago, memories of a dear friend and years spent raising our cherub babies came rushing back, relived through a recipe written in her hurried hand on a mustard yellow scrap of paper. It was titled "Cheesecakes." The recipe is sweet, simple, and purely delightful— just how I remember Jackie.

Jackie's Cheesecakes

Makes 12 individual cakes

INGREDIENTS:

1 egg

$\frac{1}{2}$ cup sugar

$\frac{1}{2}$ teaspoon almond extract

8 ounces softened cream cheese

2 tablespoons melted butter

Graham crackers

DIRECTIONS: Add first four ingredients into a bowl and beat until filling is pourable, then set aside. Combine the graham cracker crumbs and melted butter, then press into ramekin or cupcake pan, completely covering bottoms. Pour in cream cheese mixture. Bake at 375º F for 12 minutes. Let cool, then top with fruit, or drizzle with chocolate or caramel. Garnish with crushed nuts.

If there's a takeaway from my memories of Jackie, a lesson of some sort to be gained, it's simply this: Food connects us. We celebrate with food, show love through it, and share ourselves around it. Jackie is missed and remembered for so many qualities, but what brought back these recollections of our time together was a handwritten recipe of a simple dessert. When she shared her recipe with me it seemed so casual, even a little hurried and brushed aside. "Oh, it's so easy," she said. "Here." She eagerly jotted it down and passed it to me. I put it in my diaper bag and later taped it under "Desserts" in my recipe book. I've come to realize that what she was also giving me was a piece of herself, a little secret, one of her success stories.

Recipe Collection

HERE'S TO CREATING YOUR OWN!

When I was starting out in my new kitchen, I asked the best cooks in my family for their recipes. First, I bought a simple recipe book, and then I spent an evening or two with my mother reviewing favorite dishes from her collection. They varied from how to make mashed potatoes to her secret for making the perfect piecrust. I never took interest until I had my own kitchen and a special someone to share it. Start your recipe collection by asking the great cooks in your family to share their successes with you.

The collection you create will be as unique as you are. Start your recipe story today!

SEARCH
RECIPES

Enter key word 🔍

FRIENDS & FAMILY

Take the time to ask about the story behind the recipe. Recipes usually come with a little nugget that makes them unique. They may even be tied to a rich family tradition or have a deep regional backdrop. Once, while baking a lemon Jell-O cake with my Nana, I learned the recipe was a hand-me-down from my Aunt Willie Mae. It was the first time I'd heard of her, which led to more questions and more stories. I learned to listen closely, knowing I'd be called upon someday to pass them on.

Since then, I always write the name of the person who shared the recipe and the year along with the recipe. That first recipe book I purchased included an extra line titled, "A favorite of _____." At the time, I wasn't convinced that this information was necessary, but the passing of time has offered a different conclusion. This collection is more than just mine—it's a collaboration of our family favorites. Documenting this information adds a layer to each recipe's story. You'll be glad for the layers as the years go by and memories fade.

Family and friend recipes take time to acquire, because you'll likely gain them gradually as you come across a special dish at an event or celebration. If you are just getting started, spend some time with your mother or mother-in-law (a great way to learn your husband's favorites) in order to start your collection.

Never hesitate to ask for a recipe when you come across an unexpected pleasure. See it as a little treasure worth keeping—like friends and fond memories.

I met someone at a bridesmaid's luncheon who said she gifted her betrothed nieces a baking dish filled with recipe cards of the menu served at their bridesmaid luncheons. I found this a sweet and thoughtful gesture, as often the dishes served are tried and true favorites from the closest of friends—the hosts of the party. I offered similar gifts to my sisters-in-law upon their first Christmas as part of our family. I started by gathering our traditional recipes, the ones that showed up on our holiday table, and those from my mother's collection. I then added each of my brothers' best loved recipes and wrapped them in a baking dish with matching dish towels. Not only was it meant as a welcoming to the family, but it was also the gift of inside information—like offering them the other team's playbook.

New Friends, New Finds

The best thing about collecting party recipes is finding a reason to use them. Some culinary treasures come by way of your dearest friends.

MyTip: Never stop reinventing your recipe collection. Look for new twists and ideas on entertaining.

One Saturday night, new friends invited us over for appetizers, kind of a "meet the neighbors" gathering under the guise of a sporting event. We were welcomed in and immediately led to the kitchen, where an enticing spread of gourmet goodies layered the granite island, flanked by a simmering pot of homemade vegetable soup and a plate of buttered cornbread. The atmosphere was festive, the aroma intoxicating. A tray of bubbling-hot, stuffed mushrooms piqued my interest as I watched our host place them on a tray and offer them for sampling. I'll be honest, my appetizer recipe collection is rather lacking as I tend to focus on entrées, salads, and desserts, but after witnessing the casual atmosphere of a party wrapped around heavy hors d'oeuvres, combined with the ease created by a relaxed host, I'm changing my game plan. For years, I've been in search of a great stuffed mushroom recipe for my collection. While there are many to choose from, this one stands out for a reason: It has fewer ingredients, simple instructions, superior flavor, and impressive presentation. Be sure to try the Stuffed Mushrooms recipe I scored at the party.

Artichoke Dip

Ingredients:

14-ounce can artichoke hearts

1 cup water chestnuts

1 cup mayonnaise

1 cup grated Parmesan

Hot sauce TOBASCO

Paprika

Salt & Pepper

Serves: **8** Prep Time: **20 minutes**

Directions: Drain and chop artichoke hearts and water chestnuts. In an 8" x 8" oven-safe dish combine artichoke hearts, water chestnuts, mayo, and grated Parmesan (reserving some for topping). TOBASCO, salt & pepper to taste. Add remaining Parmesan and top with paprika. Bake at 350ºF until bubbling. (Approx. 20 minutes)

Stuffed Mushrooms

Ingredients:

1 pound chub spicy pork sausage

16 ounces cream cheese

Large container fresh small white mushroom caps with stems

Serves: **8** Prep Time: **20 minutes**

Directions: Brown sausage in pan. Clean mushrooms with damp paper towel. Remove stems, chop and add stems to sausage. Once sausage is fully cooked, add cream cheese, stirring until it melts. Place caps on cookie sheet and fill with sausage mixture. Bake at 350ºF for 10 minutes, or until bubbly and slightly brown. Serve hot.

RECIPE COLLECTION

The All Too Obvious Internet

No one needs to remind your generation that you have a billion cookbooks in the palm of your hands. But to find a good recipe in the sea of the internet, it helps if someone points you to quality harbors.

I'm a big fan of FoodNetwork.com. They've compiled more than 23 million recipes, categorized them according to level of difficulty, and offer a user-friendly smart phone app. One of my favorites is a shrimp and grits recipe from Bobby Flay's collection. It lives up to its 5-star rating and is an easy dish to make. Download the app, and give it a try.

When you have a unique need (someone asks you to bring a gluten- and dairy-free dessert to the dinner party) try one of my favorite sites.

Allrecipes.com bills itself as "the world's largest food-focused social network," which means the recipes come from other cooks. Search it, make it, save it, and then share it. Often the recipes include special instructions or tricks from the recipe's contributor. Found an amazing recipe to try? Follow the contributor to see what else he or she is posting. Another amazing feature is the ability to search for recipes by ingredients. Say you want to make dinner but only have a few ingredients on hand. Enter them in the search bar and see what recipes pop up, possibly saving you a trip to the store. Save favorite recipes from the site to avoid searching again. Increase your skill by joining the Allrecipes cooking school for a small monthly subscription fee, or choose the annual fee and cut the cost in half.

Yummly.com offers a similar format of recipes via social network as it boasts "recipes from the web's best foodies," but it limits your search time with some excellent filters. Some of the filters include allergies, diet, nutrition, cuisine, holiday, technique, and cook time. These filters save valuable time when searching for just the right recipe. Let's say you enter a search for Chicken Marsala, and fifty recipes pop up. You want one that's gluten-free, fewer than 400 calories, and can be accomplished in less than 30 minutes. Enter those requests in the handy filters, and now you are only searching through three recipes. What's truly unique about this site is the ability to exclude ingredients. If you have an aversion to mustard, as the founder does, you can exclude the offending ingredient as well, and limit your search that way.

Need a recipe?
Google it.
Got a recipe?
Pin it.

Pinterest

Ever visit a restaurant and enjoy a dish so much you had to have the recipe? You can try, but chances are they won't share it. Pinterest will. It's a great resource for trending recipes and the coveted copycat. Try searching by restaurant and item, such as PF Chang's Lettuce Wraps or Chipotle's Cilantro Lime Rice. Someone with a great palette has taken the time to deconstruct the dish and put it in recipe form—I bet you can't tell it apart from the original.

Grocery Stores

I love that today's modern food markets encourage cooking at home with in-store demonstration kiosks equipped with sample kitchens. We had a little wager going in our home. Early on, my husband liked to hint at what he was in the mood for before dinner each evening. I subscribe to the idea that he's in the mood for whatever I'm cooking. Case in point: the grocery store's "Gotcha Kitchen." Upon entering your grocery, you'll be enticed by a savory aroma coming from the store's sample kitchen. It's already too late—you're hooked. Suddenly, you're in the mood for whatever they're cooking. I use that same method at home—he steps into the kitchen, gets one whiff and he's onboard.

Kudos to the local grocer as their recipes are simple, usually healthy, and all the ingredients have been assembled for easy pick-up. It's a great way to demonstrate how easy preparing recipes at home can be. Granted, they've taken care of the planning steps for you, but I'll cover those later in the *Cooking Simple* chapter.

Social Gatherings

Don't ever hesitate to ask for a recipe when you come across something unexpectedly tasty at a dinner party, picnic, tailgate, barbecue, or brunch. First, the recipes serve as a memorable record of good times with great people. And second, simply by asking, you are offering the sincerest of compliments to the cook.

Magazines

If you're longing to embrace the season, I find cooking and home magazines are a great way to inspire the inner cook or cure a craving, such as apple crisp on a chilly night. Choose one that closely matches your lifestyle, or the one you hope to emulate, and order a subscription. You'll find the timely arrival of the magazine is a step ahead of the

approaching season or holiday, further spurring your creativity. Living in the South, my favorites are *Garden & Gun* and *Southern Living*, but to keep in step with my lifestyle, I also subscribe to *Cooking Light* and *life:beautiful*.

Cookbooks

I've saved this category for last because it's the expensive place to look for a recipe, and the most challenging due to the sea of cookbooks on the market today—each promising a unique spin. If you already have a cookbook idea in mind, such as Louisiana-style cooking, you can narrow your choice. But even then, you'll have to sift through the various styles from Cajun to Creole and the plethora of celebrity chef authors. So, how do you wade through all there is to offer? I look for cookbooks that inspire me, and then pull from the individual style of the author to craft my own culinary flair.

Avoid frustration and disappointment as you search for a cookbook by staying within these guidelines.

This cookbook:

• **Motivates, and energizes me to cook**
• **Meets my level of expertise**
• **Matches my lifestyle and diet**
• **Isn't a fad**

My First

Better Homes & Gardens New Cook Book was my first. It was so well thought of at the time, (pre-internet), that it was given to me as a shower present by my Nana. She, being the most esteemed cook in our family, deemed it: "The must-have cookbook for every new cook." It was nicknamed the "Red and White" because of its gingham cover resembling a tablecloth. Today's Red and White still comes as a printed three-ring notebook, but now a Kindle version is available. Every trending recipe you could possibly need to be a success in the kitchen is in there. It's simple, easy-to-follow directions allowed me to venture out and try new recipes. I always found it reassuring because the inside flap held handy bits of information such as weights and measurements, internal temperature guides for cooking meat, emergency substitutions, and ingredient equivalents. I can't tell you how many times I referred to the Red and White while learning to cook.

Glamour-ous Cooking

On the heels of the Red and White, I suppose I was looking for something less utilitarian and more romantic as a young bride—a cookbook that could be instrumental in shaping the kind of marriage I envisioned. I found it in *Glamour's Gourmet on the Run*, by Jane Kirby, *Glamour's* food editor. It opened up my world

Look for a keepsake cookbook from your honeymoon travels as a reminder of the memories and romance.

RECIPE *QuickStart*

**Cooking Skill Level . . .
What's yours?**

☐ **I can make cereal.**

☐ **I cook from boxes.**

☐ **I flambé, sauté, whatever.**

Do you own a cookbook?

☐ **No.**

☐ **Yes.**

☐ **I wrote a cookbook.**

Does cooking ever intimidate you?

☐ **I'm shaking already.**

☐ **If it's from scratch.**

☐ **My chef's hat is taller than yours.**

Thanks for your *QuickStart* answers. Now that I know you a little better, I've hand-picked a cookbook just for you. See what we've chosen at:

OurNewlywedKitchen.com.

to romance via the kitchen. In it I began to see new ways to celebrate our life together. Suddenly, a lazy Saturday morning was transformed into something more as I glanced at the photo of Eggs Benedict served on a tray with cloth napkins and a daisy in a bud vase. A weeknight dinner became cozier when the cookbook authors titled it *Potato and Leek Soup in Bread Bowls.* The ingredients they listed were fresher than those previously known to me—the flavors entirely unexpected. I found success in my new ability to turn the ordinary into the extraordinary. While the Red and White was a valuable tool, *Glamour* provided a vision. You'll need both the vision and tools as you build your kitchen and enrich your marriage.

MyTip: *If you're inclined to buy a cookbook, visit your local library to check one out. If you find yourself reluctant to return it, you may have found a keeper.*

Do you have a refined interest in food and seek the cooking experience as a hobby? Maybe your diet is limited to vegan or vegetarian, or restricted by gluten or dairy free. Are you focused on exercise and slimming down? Do health concerns direct you toward better nutrition and whole foods? Or do you live in a region known for its unique cuisine? These are a few examples where a lifestyle cookbook could be very beneficial.

Lifestyle Cookbooks

Regretfully, eating healthy hasn't always been a priority for me, even though it was patterned for me as a child. The problem was the definition of *healthy* kept changing. I found it challenging to keep up with the fads. The cookbook that addressed my much sought-after lifestyle and promised to untangle the ever-changing controversy over healthy food was *The Real Food Diet Cookbook* by Dr. Josh Axe. It became my go-to guide. The recipes were helpful, but I gleaned the most from the training on nutrients versus calories, what foods to purchase organic, and the safe-cooking section that guided me away from toxic nonstick pots and pans.

I like Axe's perspective that food is medicine: What we put in our bodies directly affects how we feel, as well as how we carry out our daily tasks, responsibilities, and life-goals—our well-being so to speak. It's difficult to pursue God's path for our lives when we don't feel our best.

The responsibility of our family's nutritional intake weighing heavily on me, I began to consider the effects that processed foods were playing on our health. With a new distrust toward processed and fast food, I gradually turned to real food such as raw spinach and greens, and local, organic, farm-raised meat and eggs.

Our grown children, through my example, adopted a focus on health and nutrition—an achievement, since I aimed to pass on my new knowledge to the next generation. As that responsibility waned, a new aim emerged toward slowing the aging process for my husband and me. We want to be healthy enough to keep up with our children and ongoing life goals. The result was an even greater interest in nutrition and exercise for both of us.

I've noticed our health focus to be more successful and budget-friendly when our kitchen is equipped with safe, nontoxic cooking tools; fully stocked with healthy ingredients; and armed with recipes that support our nutritional goals and cravings. But this is my lifestyle story. While I believe health and nutrition to be a worthy goal to pursue, my point is for you to find your own lifestyle cookbook together, and to embrace your kitchen, building successes through it. ❦

Take care of yourselves for each other's sake.

SPRING

Look to the first spring bud, warm summer breeze, crisp autumn

FALL

SUMMER

color, and frosty winter morn for your recipe inspirations.

WINTER

Favorite recipes can bind you to a special place and time.

Start your keepsake recipe collection below. For more printable recipe pages go to **OurNewlywedKitchen.com**.

Recipe Linguini with Clam Sauce

Ingredients:

8 oz linguini
½ cup olive oil
3 Tbsp butter
1 medium Onion, chopped
2 cloves garlic, minced
1 lb chopped clams with juice - can or frozen
2 Tbsp fresh basil or 2 tsp dried
¼ cup minced fresh parsley
Grated Parmeson cheese

Serves: 2-3 **Prep Time:** 30 min

From:
A Favorite of: Mom & Dad

Directions:

Cook linguini according to package direction
In large skillet, heat oil and butter.
Add Onion and garlic, saute over medium heat 1-2 min
Stir in clams, basil and parsley.
Heat to desired temperature. Careful not to over boil
Serve clam sauce over linguini
Sprinkle cheese on top.

OurNewlywedKitchen.com

Recipe Chicken Pot Pie 425°F

Ingredients: 2 pie crusts

2-3 stalks of Celery
2-3 carrots,
1 onion
½ head of califlour
2 chicken thighs/ 1 breast
1 can Condensed cream of chicken
(or celery, mushroom, etc.)

Serves: 3-4 **Prep Time:** 30 prep 30-45 bake **From:** Mom
A Favorite of: Matthew

Directions: Chop vegetables. Boil Chicken.
Combine in bowl w/ can of soup.
Baking pie pans - put 1 crust in, fill, top & cover.
Add slits to center.
Bake 30-45 min, or until golden brown.
Let rest 10 min before serving.

OurNewlywedKitchen.com

Recipe — EGGPLANT PARMESAN

Ingredients:

- 1 Eggplant
- 2 eggs
- breadcrumbs
- 1½ jar of pasta sauce
- Spaghetti / Angel hair
- 1 lb mozzarella
- grated parmesan
- basil leaves

From:

A Favorite of:

Serves:_____ Prep Time:_____

Directions:

OurNewlywedKitchen.com

Recipe — SPINACH RICOTTA-STUFFED CHICKEN

Ingredients:

- 10 ounces spinach
- ½ cup ricotta
- 2 cloves garlic (chopped)
- 4 chicken thighs
- 4 roma tomatoes
- 2 onions

From:

A Favorite of:

Serves: 4 Prep Time:_____

Directions:

OurNewlywedKitchen.com

Recipe — Acorn Squash Soup

Ingredients:

- 1 acorn squash
- 2-3 small red onions
- 1 can coconut milk
- olive oil
- cinnamon
- nutmeg

From:

A Favorite of:

Serves: 4-6 Prep Time: 1 hr

Directions:

OurNewlywedKitchen.com

Finding the right recipes to fit your lifestyle can be time-consuming. Use these guidelines to quickly assess which recipes work best for you.

Recipe Filter

Here's a checklist to use as you try a new recipe. Keep these ideas in mind and you'll save yourself a ton of headaches.

- Is the recipe within our skill level?
- Does it look like something we will enjoy eating?
- Does it meet our lifestyle or dietary guidelines?
- Does it fit our budget?
- Do we recognize all the ingredients?
- Are the ingredients easy to find (in season)?
- Are any of the ingredients in our pantry or fridge?
- Do we recognize the terms used? (sauté, braise, fold)
- Do we have all the tools necessary to prepare the meal?
- Will we have enough time to prep and cook this recipe?

Does it sound yummy?

When reading a recipe, try to put the flavors and textures together in your mind. With practice, you will begin to imagine great pairings. I can recall the first time I made a fresh blueberry sauce as a topping for crepes with vanilla ice cream. It was remarkable—really something special. I was familiar with blueberries, so I could picture them in a rich and sweet warm sauce, but there was something different after I tasted it that set it apart. It was the lemon juice. It countered the sugar for an explosive taste sensation. Now, when I see a recipe where blueberries meet lemon juice, I know it'll be a perfect pairing.

MyTip: *Some dishes are a little easier to imagine if a photo is included, but learn to rely on your taste buds—trust them and practice pairings as you go.*

Am I skilled enough to try this?

It's important to become successful at basic skills before trying advanced ones. When
I was a child, Aunt Ouie served as my reading tutor. She deterred me from choosing a
book that was above my reading level for fear I would become frustrated and give up
on reading altogether. She wanted me to love reading, so she taught me to determine my
comprehension level by reading the first page of a book and holding up a finger every time
I came to a word I didn't recognize. If I held up five fingers by the end of the page, the book
was too difficult. I think the same principle can be applied to new recipes and novice cooks.
And I do want you to love cooking!

I remembered my aunt's advice one afternoon while discussing recipes with my
daughter, Elise, and her friend Lindsey, both confident cooks. Lindsey tries one or two new
recipes a month on average, making sure they contain no more than one new ingredient.
She's careful to stay within her skill level but explores new recipes to avoid the rut. You can
determine for yourself the number of unfamiliar ingredients, tools, or terms that add up
before you ditch the recipe.

Personally, I'm with Lindsey. More than one unfamiliar ingredient, tool, or term in a single recipe, and I move on.

It's worthwhile to stretch your knowledge, but as the unfamiliar items add up, the fun factor goes down, and the chance for frustration, waste, and inconvenience increases dramatically.

Do we recognize the ingredients?

Once in a while you'll come across a recipe with an ingredient you don't recognize. I feel a little silly admitting it now, but cream of tartar was that ingredient for me. I've come to realize its importance in the baking process, as it stabilizes the egg whites in meringues allowing them to get that toasty look after baking. For that reason, I keep it on the shelf. But I still find I avoid recipes that contain it, or seek out those with an alternative ingredient. Sorry, cream of tartar, you still sound intimidating. Continuing to introduce unfamiliar ingredients to your meals is one way to avoid getting into a rut in the kitchen. Yes, it can be intimidating at first. An easy way to accomplish this is to temporarily subscribe to a pre-packaged dinner delivery plan. The exact amount you'll need for the recipe is included, so there's no waste in buying more than you need or space taken up in your pantry or fridge if you didn't enjoy it.

Are the ingredients easy to find (in season)?

It's frustrating to plan a menu and run to the store with list in hand, only to learn the store doesn't carry the ingredient, or it's out of stock. Some complicated dishes have ingredients so obscure that they may require a trip to a specialized market. I certainly don't want to discourage your adventurous spirit, but being able to locate specialty ingredients such as furikake (Japanese seasoning) will be a large part of your success. Before you get your heart set on making a dish with an ingredient that's foreign to you, do a little homework—find out if you can get your hands on it.

Does it fit our budget?

If you want to be a budget-conscious cook, you'll consider the cost of a recipe's ingredients. I rarely prepare a true Beef Bourguignon because of the cost of the meat. I typically try to stay economical, unless it's a holiday or celebration, but even then there are ways to cut costs. For example, if you love rib eye steak, look for holiday sales on a standing rib roast and have your butcher cut it into rib eye steaks to freeze for later. The savings can be significant. If the recipe lists expensive spices or dry marinades, consider how many times the ingredient can be used dividing the cost per use. Pricey ingredients such as poppy seeds and saffron are good examples because a little goes a long way. Avoid letting them sit on the shelf by finding other recipes that use those same spices.

MyTip: *To prevent waste, invest in expensive ingredients only after you've tasted the recipe at a restaurant or friend's home and determined it was a meal you would serve again and again.*

Are the ingredients already in our kitchen?

Flour, sugar, canned tomatoes, pasta, rice, potatoes, chicken broth, chicken breasts, ground beef, and olive oil are staples I routinely purchase. You'll find the recipes you're drawn to will most likely determine what become your staples. Choosing recipes that include staples promotes buying them in bulk, which helps you stay on budget. These recipes become real lifesavers when you're tired, out of groceries, or your plans change. In a pinch, you'll always have a "rescue meal" on hand.

Do we recognize the terminology?

This isn't a big deal with Google at your fingertips. A foreign term is actually an opportunity to learn something new, as long as you don't get in over your head. Keep it simple. If you don't understand what blanching or folding means, look it up and try something new—but try one technique at a time. You'll find yourselves opening up new skill areas within your cooking experience.

Do we have the tools we'll need?

Most likely you do, but double-check before starting. If you're short a tool, consider substituting with something similar before purchasing. I subscribe to the idea that less is more in the kitchen drawer. For example, in my recipe for rigatoni it calls for a deep baking dish, but can a 9"x13" be used? Of course. See page 61 for the tools list.

Does it meet our lifestyle and diet?

This is a hard one for me, because I so dearly value the recipes passed down by my family—childhood favorites, as well as dishes prepared for celebrations and holidays. Today, as I run them through my current recipe filter, I've found they don't always match my health-conscious lifestyle. So, I've struck a balance between making those trusted recipes healthier (reducing fat, sugar, salt) and updating my collection with fresh, lean, organic, and gluten-free versions.

Do we have enough time to prep and cook this?

I learned this lesson the hard way. Upon traveling home from honeymooning in Germany, my new husband craved Sauerbraten. I bought all the ingredients and began to prep and cook our meal while he sat waiting in anticipation. Moments later when I read all the way through the recipe, I realized the meat takes 72 hours to marinate! Sauerbraten literally translates to pickled roast meat. Needless to say, we dined out that night.

If you covet your downtime, steer toward recipes that take 30 minutes or less from prep to table. Don't overlook the slow cooker as a great place to save time in the kitchen. A quick prep, and the slow cooker does the rest.

Always, always read all the way through the recipe before you start making it.

Our Newlywed
KITCHEN

· COOKING SIMPLE ·

Turbulence!

"I hate turbulence," I blurted out, not realizing how loudly I was talking. My ears were plugged due to the plane's changing cabin pressure. I was speaking in the general direction of the young woman sitting next to me, my hands clinging to both armrests.

"This seems a little worse to me than usual," I gasped as we bounced and lurched in our seats. "Yes," she said. "It does."

"I don't even like to fly. Do you?"

"Well, I'm a flight attendant, so I don't mind it, usually."

She was flying standby to Chicago to meet up with her fiancé, which explained why she wasn't wearing a uniform.

Great, I thought, *Even the flight attendant is a little nervous.*

Rather than fixate on my fears, I chose to placate them by engaging her in conversation. Sometimes I use communication as a soothing agent, so I leaned in and grilled her with questions.

Angela was lovely and soft-spoken. She told me about her fiancé, how they'd met, and that they had been dating for almost two years. Sharing that he had proposed just a few weeks earlier, she presented her hand complete with a fresh manicure and adorned with a glistening ring. Her fiancé already owned a beautiful home, and she would soon be moving to his state.

All of this information flowed from her lips in one long, enthusiastic monologue. I was so thankful for the distraction but also immersed in the pure romance of her story. Then she paused, appearing somewhat forlorn. "What's wrong?" I asked, urging her to go on. After a moment, she quietly divulged her predicament. Her angst was real and her plight impending. She announced that his parents were coming in for the holidays, and she was panicked at the expectation of preparing dinner for them.

It's odd what contributes to our individual fears and intimidations. At 30,000 feet, nauseous from being bounced and jolted, desperately trying to ignore the flashing lights and the repeated weather updates from the pilot, I found myself a white-knuckled bundle of keenly focused nerves. She, on the other hand, seemed unaware of the rather turbulent circumstances surrounding us. Instead, what got her wide-eyed and considerably anxious was an approaching dinner party for people who couldn't help but love her.

Fear can be brought on by a lack of control or a lack of knowledge. I so wanted to lift her from her threatening dilemma as her phobia happened to be one of my strengths.

"It'll be all right. I'll help you."

"But you don't understand," she said, clearly flustered, "I don't know how to cook at all. I don't know any of it."

I asked if she had ever spent any time in the kitchen growing up. She said she would have liked to, but her mother didn't cook. She went on to say that the books and magazines she pored over made cooking look like a hopeless task, one she could never master. She was even skeptical that anybody actually lived the way it appeared in the magazines.

We landed in Chicago safely, exchanged email addresses, and said our good-byes, promising to get together soon. Over the next couple of weeks I sent her a few emails containing recipes—tried-and-true favorites from my family's table—and included a grocery list of the items she needed to have on hand before I arrived for our cooking lesson.

On the arranged date, Angela invited me in and showed me around her charming, soon-to-be home. We prepared three meals and a dessert together, all the while talking about setting the table, timing the meal, plating and serving, and the value of bringing the family together around the table, in her case, with her soon-to-be in-laws.

As we cleaned up and I prepared to leave, she graciously thanked me. And then she noted that when she was growing up, her family didn't have a regular practice of eating together around a table. Their mealtime was mostly chaotic. Someone was always getting up from the table to retrieve something: a drink, a fork, the ketchup, the phone. Most of the time, they were walking their plate into the living room so they could eat in front of the television.

On my drive home, I began to reflect on her family's mealtime experience. It was either full-on commotion or nonexistent, and I was suddenly reminded of the first words I spoke to Angela on the plane, "I hate turbulence!"

A PRAYER FOR
Confidence

from
_____

....
....
....
....
....
....
....
....
....
....
....
....
....

2 CORINTHIANS: 7:16 ESV

I REJOICE, BECAUSE I HAVE COMPLETE CONFIDENCE IN YOU.

The kitchen can be an intimidating place for some people. When a lack of knowledge is coupled with an expectation for perfection, fears can mount. If you suffer from self-doubt around all things kitchen, remember, cooking is not about perfection, it's about the nurturing you're providing. Look to store displays, magazine spreads, and Pinterest pins as sources of inspiration, not intimidation. Take it slow, appreciate the process of learning, and know that you are capable of making good meals.

Cooking Simple

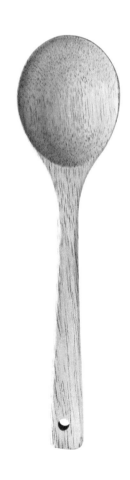

Before you turn the page, let's all get on the same one. Cooking is work. I'm making that truthful statement so your expectations are within reach. There is a sophisticated food culture out there promising effortless, quick, and gourmet meals. It's not deceptive really, it just lacks the whole story. As a typical couple, you're not outfitted with a crew to shop, chop, mop, and organize your kitchen for you. No recipe is quick if you don't have the ingredients on hand, or effortless if you don't own the proper tools for the task. Cooking becomes quick after you've made recipes numerous times and are familiar with your kitchen and tools. "Quick" cooking is a skill that takes time to develop.

I'm going to be really straight with you. After years of making meals for my family, I can look back and recognize the advantage to home cooking that may not occur to newlyweds. I started cooking because of my strong desire to nurture and a great need to save money. But then I discovered the other, less tangible fruits of my labor, and that's what I'm passionate about sharing with you. When we gather around a table, share a meal, and pray together, unity happens, comfort is given, and joy is found. Around the table, a marriage is strengthened, children feel a sense of belonging, and health is established. Yes, it's work, but the result is so worthwhile. Now, it's up to you to decide: Do you want to invest in a routine that can produce such valuable dividends?

TERMS YOU'LL NEED TO KNOW

Recipe: A list of ingredients and cooking instructions for the preparation of one specific dish

Menu: The listing of the paired dishes to be served together—a main dish, side dish(es), and/or dessert. A complete menu doesn't need to include all of these, but a good menu will contain a balance of food groups.

Food pairing: The art of combining complementary foods based on: taste (sweet, sour, salty, bitter, umami/savory), texture (crisp, creamy, etc.), color, and aroma

Prepping: The gathering of all ingredients and tools for the process of preparing food to be cooked. On your counter, place a bowl to collect debris, eliminating multiple trips to the garbage or compost. When cutting meat and vegetables, set up two dedicated cutting boards, and knives. If you don't have two, prep all vegetables first, followed by meat, poultry, or fish. Be careful that the raw juices from uncooked meat don't contaminate other food. Clean up immediately by washing hands, cutting boards, knives, and countertops with hot soapy water.

Timing: Before prepping or cooking, it's important to assess the time it will take to create each recipe, because this will determine which task to start first. Dinner will be ready within the timeframe of the recipe that requires the most amount of time to prep and cook. Start that dish first, then begin other dishes while the first is cooking. Your goal is to have each menu item at the correct temperature, ready to be served at the same time.

Plating: The styling and arranging of food as it pertains to the plate prior to serving. If the plate is your canvas, think of the lip as the frame—don't overcrowd the plate. White dinnerware is trending because it's a great backdrop to most food. Dark-toned dinnerware will accent light-colored food, e.g., rice and potatoes. Or, select dinnerware representing seasonal colors as a change of pace. Create interest by using different vessels as plates. Use a small dipping bowl to hold spiced apples. Arrange food in odd numbers. Three or five shrimp look better on a plate than two or four. Create height by stacking or layering foods. Try placing your protein on top of a bed of mashed potatoes, and lay asparagus spears across the top. Garnish for color, texture, or aroma. Be sure the garnish complements the meal's flavor.

Therefore encourage one another and build one another up, just as you are doing.

1 THESSALONIANS 5:11 ESV

Menu Planning
& Pairing

If there is an art to planning a menu, then my Nana was Rembrandt.

Nana outlined for me the basic mediums to work within—taste, texture, color, and aroma—while pairing the basic food families of proteins, starches, and vegetables.

She taught me to use all of my senses when planning what to cook. She explained that because we first eat with our eyes, we should look to vegetables for pops of color on our canvas—the plate.

From Nana, I learned to create interest for the palate by serving a combination of different textures, for example, flaky salmon with creamy mashed potatoes and a side of crunchy fresh asparagus. For an unexpected flavor twist, Nana sometimes paired savory main menu items with sweet, such as roast beef with maple glazed carrots and fluffy angel biscuits. Finally, she taught me to garnish with fresh-cut herbs and citrus because of their color and aromatic qualities.

A Broad-brush Approach

Refresh the Palate

Within your weekly menu, try to avoid the duplication of the same proteins, starches, and vegetables in back-to-back meals. Why? The similar flavor components cause palate fatigue. Instead, think "palate refresh" when planning for the week or month. Add variety by choosing different proteins (chicken, fish, beef, beans, tofu) combined with various colored vegetables and starches (brown rice, sweet potatoes). Create even more interest by adding international flavors, lighter meatless meals, and one-pot dishes. Alternating cooking techniques by using a wok, griddle, grill, or cast iron skillet also adds variety to the menu.

Create Versatility

Consider the versatility of a simple bag of potatoes. They can be baked, mashed, boiled, roasted with olive oil and rosemary, seared on a griddle with onions and peppers, fried as a side to pair with shiitake mushroom burgers, chilled in a salad for a Saturday picnic, or scalloped with Gruyére cheese in a casserole. Mastering the many ways one ingredient can be prepared helps you create diversity in your meal plans. A great place to start implementing this strategy is with the Italian red sauce. It opens the door to spaghetti, rigatoni, manicotti, lasagna, and other meal options.

View your weekly meal plan as a game of fill-in-the-blanks.

Dollars & Sense

Steward those dollars well by looking for sales on meat, especially before and after a holiday. Ask the butcher to carve a ham, separating it into steaks and cubes, and reserving the bone (a free service offered at most grocery stores). Take the meat home and freeze it. The ham steaks pair beautifully with macaroni and cheese. Planning to go on a picnic? Throw the cubes in a food processor for ham salad sandwiches, or make up two baking dishes of ham and scalloped potatoes, one for dinner and the other to share with a friend in need. Remember that ham bone? Put it in a slow cooker with Great Northern beans, toss in a few garlic cloves and mirepoix (diced onions, carrots, and celery), and six hours later you'll have a meal that will feed a small army.

Our Newlywed
KITCHEN

• TEST RECIPES •

Rigatoni *with Caprese Salad*

Serves: **4**

Prep Time: **30 minutes**

Meat sauce: 20 minutes

Pasta: 12 minutes

Bake Time: **30 minutes**

Ingredients:

16 ounces Rigatoni pasta

4 ounces Swiss cheese (shredded)

4 ounces Mozzarella (shredded)

1 pound ground beef

1 pound Italian sausage

2 15-ounce cans tomatoes (diced)

2 15-ounce cans tomato sauce

1 yellow onion

4 garlic cloves

1 tablespoon Italian seasoning

1 teaspoon sugar

1 teaspoon olive oil

Cooking Step by Step
Follow this order so your recipes are completed at the same time.

Pasta step 1.

Meat Sauce steps 1-4.

Pasta steps 2-3.

Meat Sauce steps 5-6.

Follow up on all remaining steps.

Directions:

Pasta

1. In a pot of water, add a drizzle of olive oil, one teaspoon of salt, and the rigatoni; cook according to package directions. **2.** When tender, drain the pasta in a colander and return it to the cooking pot (no heat). **3.** Stir in 1 to 2 ladles of sauce to add color and flavor.

Meat Sauce & Layering

1. In a large pot with lid (Dutch oven) brown meat on high heat (until browned all the way through). **2.** Add diced onion and garlic to the pot; sauté until the onion is translucent. **3.** Add tomatoes, Italian seasoning blend, and sugar to the meat mixture; stir. **4.** Cover and reduce heat to simmer. **5.** Butter a deep (4-5 inches) baking dish; cover the bottom of the dish with half of the pasta; top with half of the Swiss and Mozzarella. Repeat to make two layers (or 1 layer if using a 9x13-inch baking dish). **6.** Bake pasta at 350°F for up to 30 minutes, or until cheese is fully melted. Remove from oven; serve with sauce ladled over the top.

Pairing:

Caprese Salad

Find the recipe for Caprese salad on the next page.

We're taking you island hopping for tonight's entrée. Originating in Sicily, rigatoni means ridges and is the perfect pasta to capture all the savory sauce and bubbling cheese you'll add to it. Buon appetito!

Caprese Salad

Serves: **4**

Prep Time: **10 minutes**

Ingredients:

3 vine-ripe tomatoes

16 ounces fresh Mozzarella

16 fresh basil leaves

Extra virgin olive oil (EVOO)

Balsamic vinegar glaze
or reduction

Salt and pepper

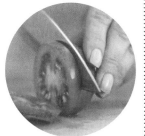

Directions:

Caprese Salad (it's as easy as *slice, slice, drizzle!*)

1. Use a serrated knife to slice mozzarella into even rounds. **2.** Place tomato on its side. With the same knife, slice off stem and bottom of the tomato, then parallel cut the remaining tomato into 5 or 6 uniform rounds. **3.** Arrange Mozzarella and tomatoes into preferred display and layer with basil leaves. **4.** Drizzle EVOO and balsamic vinegar reduction over top. **5.** Salt and pepper to taste. **6.** Serve chilled.

Named after the Isle of Capri, this combination of tomato, fresh basil, and creamy Mozzarella add a fresh and fragrant bouquet to the meal.

Thai Chicken
Jasmine Rice & Sugar Snap Peas

Serves: 4

Prep Time: 30 minutes

Chicken: 10-12 minutes
(2 batches)

Rice: 15 minutes

Sugar snap peas: 6 minutes

Ingredients:

3 boneless/skinless
chicken breasts

3 teaspoons sesame oil

1 15-ounce can coconut milk

6 tablespoons peanut butter

4 tablespoons soy sauce

4 teaspoons red curry paste

1 red bell pepper

3 scallions

1 cup Jasmine rice

1 pound sugar snap peas

Cilantro

Cooking Step by Step
*Follow this order so your recipes are
completed at the same time.*

Rice steps 1-3.

Chicken steps 1-7.

Snap peas steps 1-4.

Chicken steps 8-9.

Directions:

Jasmine Rice (Mahatma)

1. In a medium pot add 1 1/2 cups of water and bring to a boil. **2.** Stir in 1 cup of rice. (Optional: Add 1 tablespoon of butter and 1 teaspoon of salt) **3.** Cover with lid and reduce heat to low. Simmer for 15 minutes or until all water is absorbed.

Thai Chicken

1. Cut 3 chicken breasts on the diagonal in small even strips. **2.** Bring skillet to medium heat as you add 2 teaspoons of sesame oil (just enough to coat the bottom of pan). **3.** Place chicken in the pan (do not overcrowd; cook two batches if needed). Sear until lightly brown, about 3 minutes. **4.** While chicken is cooking, chop peppers and scallions, discarding pepper seeds and stems and scallion root bulb. **5.** Turn chicken and cook approximately 3 minutes; transfer to plate to avoid overcooking. **6.** In same skillet, sauté the peppers and scallions for 3 minutes. **7.** In a bowl, whisk peanut butter, soy sauce, coconut milk, and red curry paste until smooth; pour over vegetables when they are tender. **8.** Stir in chicken pieces; cook 2 to 3 minutes or until the sauce begins to bubble and turns dark caramel in color. **9.** Spoon over plated rice. Garnish with cilantro.

Sugar Snap Peas

1. Rinse. **2.** Pull stem and string from peas. **3.** In pan, heat 1 teaspoon sesame oil on medium-high, add snap peas; salt and pepper to taste. **4.** Stir occasionally for 3-5 minutes until peas are crisp yet tender.

Pairing: The peppers add a bright splash of color to the peanut sauce atop the fragrant Jasmine rice. The fresh cilantro adds aroma, and the sesame oil's subtle, nutty flavor is heightened by the heat from the red curry paste.

Salmon *Mashed Potatoes & Asparagus*

Serves: 4

Prep Time: 30 minutes

Salmon: 20 minutes

Mashed potatoes: 30 minutes

Asparagus: 15 minutes

Ingredients:

1 1/2 pounds skinless salmon fillets

3 tablespoons butter

1 lemon

4 Yukon gold potatoes

4 tablespoons milk

1 pound fresh asparagus

Salt & pepper

Cooking Step by Step
Follow this order so your recipes are completed at the same time.

Preheat oven to 450°F.

Potatoes steps 1-3.

Salmon steps 1-3.

Asparagus steps 1-3.

Follow up on all remaining steps.

Directions:

Salmon

1. Line a cookie sheet with aluminum foil, or butter a small baking dish so the salmon won't stick. **2.** Cut the salmon into four even pieces; salt and pepper to taste. **3.** Place in preheated oven. **4.** Test with fork at about 12 minutes. When it flakes in the middle, it's done. Garnish with lemon and melted butter (optional).

Mashed Potatoes

1. Rinse and peel potatoes. **2.** Quarter potatoes and place them in a large pot, covering them with cold water. Add 1 teaspoon of salt. **3.** Bring to a boil for 10 to 12 minutes. **4.** Test for tenderness with a fork; the fork should pierce but not break the potato. **5.** Drain into colander, and then place potatoes back in the pot (if using a potato masher or hand mixer) or into a bowl (if using a stand mixer). Add 2 tablespoons butter, about 4 tablespoons milk, and salt and pepper. Mash until smooth. Don't overcook potatoes or they become gluey.

Asparagus

1. Rinse. **2.** Remove the bottom fibrous part of the stalk by snapping it off; discard. **3.** In a skillet, place a 1/2 inch of water, a dash of salt, and the remaining tender stalks and spears of asparagus. **4.** Bring to medium heat; cover and steam for about 10 minutes.

MyTip: Cook potatoes right after you peel them or they will turn brown. They are still safe to eat and it won't change the taste, just the presentation. If you can't cook immediately, submerge them in water and place in the refrigerator, but no longer than overnight.

Our Newlywed KITCHEN

· 21-DINNER ROTATION ·

DINNER
Surprises Me Nightly!

Scrolling through Facebook late one afternoon before starting dinner, I came across an interesting post. It read: "Dinner surprises me nightly!" As I contemplated the phrase and clever wording of the statement, "Ditto" popped-up in the comment line below it, immediately followed by another reply, "Dinner surprises me nightly, too!" Initially amused by the avalanche of responses, I quickly surmised it was the bewitching hour when a grumble from the belly begs "What's for dinner?" I wondered how many of us, from all over the country, were asking that same question. This was an obvious plea for help, but I'd noticed other examples as well. Visit a supermarket any evening between 4:00 and 6:30 P.M., and you'll witness the desperation of hungry, tired shoppers dashing down the aisles as they try to come up with a dinner decision on the spot and standing in long checkout lines, wishing instead that they were home. If we're commiserating on Facebook about this everyday occurrence, shouldn't we search for a better plan?

Having experienced the same frustration as my Facebook friends, I devised a solution to this nightly dilemma. I started by asking myself what I wanted to accomplish with my dinner plan. I wanted to:

- Eliminate multiple trips to the grocery store
- Stay on budget by eating at home
- Increase our health by preparing the freshest meals possible

I knew it would take planning to accomplish these goals. So I crafted an efficient, budget-friendly system that enabled me to get healthy dinners on the table, quickly and consistently. It became my 21-Dinner Rotation.

If you could consistently plan healthy dinners, stay on budget, and save precious time in three simple steps, would you?

21-Dinner Rotation

Eating healthy, avoiding stress, and saving time and money are easy with my simple 21-Dinner Rotation plan. As I shaped this three-step system, I noticed we averaged 21 dinners at home per month—and that's how it became the 21-Dinner Rotation. How often do you want to, and need to, eat at home? Base your system on what fits your lifestyle.

Step One: *Your Calendar*

To get started, all you'll need is a pencil, your monthly calendar, and the free downloadable *21-Dinner Rotation Monthly Menus Calendar* and the *Grocery Grab List.* Go to: **OurNewlywedKitchen.com** to print both.

Circle the nights you plan to cook dinner this week.

April

SUN	MON	TUE	WED	THU	FRI	SAT
1	2	3	4	5	6	7
8	9	10	11	12	13	14

This is where you take control. We're starting out small with three dinners at home this week.

To illustrate this point, I've circled three sample nights you'll be dining at home for the week. The open dates are evenings you'll be dining away from home. Think fun date night, outing with friends, or the dreaded working late. You can quickly see that the evenings circled are the ones that will give you control over your health and budget.

MyTip: *As you create your 21-Dinner Rotation, remember to start small. You'll find success and build confidence with each new recipe.*

Step Two: Your Menu

Fill the circles with meals you'll cook on the three selected dates.

April

SUN	MON	TUE	WED	THU	FRI	SAT
1	2 Thai Chicken Jasmine Rice Sugar Snap Peas	3 Rigatoni Caprese Salad	4	5 Salmon Mashed Potatoes Asparagus	6	7
8	9	10	11	12	13	14

I've added the meals above from my test recipes collection. You can do the same using the collection you've started. Chances are, coming up with three meals wasn't much of a challenge for you, but what will you do for weeks two, three, and four? Fill in the questions in the sidebar for some *QuickStart* ideas.

Once you find a winning recipe, place it in your 21-Dinner Rotation collection. The more favorites you gather, the easier it is to plan and the more variety you'll have to choose from throughout the month.

Use these *QuickStart* questions as inspiration for your home-cooked meal ideas.

List three recipes you know how to cook.

What does he like to cook?

What new recipes would you like to try?

What are three of his favorite meals?

Step Three: *Your Grocery List*

Build your grocery list based on the ingredients from your three Test Recipes.

As you read the recipe's ingredients list, note which items you already have in your pantry, spice rack, fridge, and freezer. Then write the items you'll need to buy in the assigned categories on the *Grocery Grab List*. As I did on the side column, you might want to jot down ideas for breakfast, lunch, desserts, and snacks so you'll remember to include those items to your grocery list. Don't forget to add household items you'll need for the week.

All three dinner recipes and the Caprese salad recipe are located in the Cooking Simple chapter.

Thai Chicken

Jasmine Rice | Sugar Snap Peas
Serves 4

---

3 boneless/skinless chicken breasts
3 teaspoons sesame oil
1 15-ounce can coconut milk
6 tablespoons peanut butter
4 tablespoons soy sauce
4 teaspoons red curry paste
1 red bell pepper
3 scallions
1 cup Jasmine rice
8 ounces sugar snap peas

Rigatoni

Caprese Salad
Serves 4

---

16 ounces rigatoni pasta
4 ounces Swiss cheese, shredded
4 ounces Mozzarella cheese, shredded
1 pound ground beef
1 pound Italian sausage
2 15-ounce cans diced tomatoes
2 15-ounce cans tomato sauce
1 yellow onion
4 garlic cloves
1 tablespoon Italian seasoning
1 teaspoon sugar
1 tomato
Fresh Mozzarella ball
8 basil leaves
Balsamic glaze
EVOO

Salmon

Mashed Potatoes | Asparagus
Serves 4

---

1 1/2 pounds skinless salmon fillets
1 tablespoon butter
1 lemon
8 small potatoes
3 tablespoons milk
2 tablespoons butter
1 bunch fresh asparagus

Grocery Grab!

Produce
red bell pepper

scallions

sugar snap peas

1 bag yellow onions

garlic

1 tomato

asparagus

1 lemon

fresh basil

1 bag small potatoes

blueberries

apples

Meat/Seafood
3 boneless chicken breasts

1 pound ground beef

1 pound Italian sausage

1 1/2 pounds skinless salmon

Dairy
8 ounces Swiss shredded

8 ounces Mozzarella shredded

Mozzarella ball   butter

milk   eggs

Dry Groceries
Jasmine rice

16-ounce box rigatoni

Italian blend seasoning

salt & pepper

cereal

popcorn

pita chips

Canned & Jarred
sesame oil

coconut milk

soy sauce

crunchy peanut butter

red chile paste

olive oil

2 cans diced tomato

2 cans tomato sauce

Balsamic glaze

honey

mustard

Bakery
5-grain bread

Deli
sliced turkey

Provolone cheese

hummus

Frozen
frozen yogurt

Beverages
tea

Personal

Household

Pets

Breakfast ideas
cereal and milk

eggs

blueberries

tea and honey

Lunch ideas
sandwiches

apples

Dessert ideas
frozen yogurt

Snack ideas
popcorn

pita chips

hummus

Grocery List Notables:

Many of the items listed on this sample grocery list will be used multiple times before you need to buy them again. To truly optimize the budget angle of this system, find other recipes that contain these items or simply repeat the recipes again during the month.

Why cooking at home makes a difference to your budget and waistline.

COST AND CALORIES COMPARISON

POPULAR RESTAURANT	*YOUR HOMEMADE*
SPAGHETTI WITH SALAD	**SPAGHETTI WITH SALAD**
881 calories per serving	502 calories per serving
Serves 2	Serves 8
$42.00 (with tax and tip)	$22.27 (with leftovers)
$21.00 per serving	$2.78 per serving

A savings of $36.44 to eat at home with 379 fewer calories!

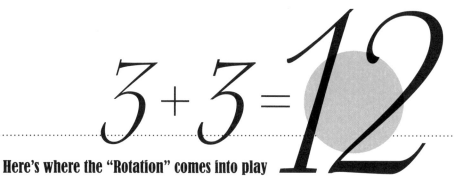

3 + 3 = 12

Here's where the "Rotation" comes into play

It's curious math, but stay with me. You've been introduced to three sample recipes for the first week of the month (Thai Chicken, Rigatoni, Salmon). Now, I'm going to challenge you to come up with three more for week two. Note: If you get stuck turn back to the *QuickStart* questions for recipe ideas. I've inserted three of my personal "keepers" below:

- Pork chops with blackberry sauce, sweet potatoes, and green beans
- Chicken Marsala with linguini pasta and broccoli florets
- Beef tacos with pinto beans and cilantro lime rice

You can find these recipes and more at OurNewlywedKitchen.com.

April

SUN	MON	TUE	WED	THU	FRI	SAT
1	2 Thai Chicken Jasmine Rice Sugar Snap Peas	3 Rigatoni w/ Meat Sauce Caprese Salad	4	5 Salmon Mashed Potatoes Asparagus	6	7
8	9 Pork Chops Blackberry Sauce Sweet Potatoes Fresh Green Beans	10 Chicken Marsala Linguini Pasta Broccoli	11	12 Beef Tacos, Pinto Beans, Cilantro Lime Rice, Guac & Chips	13	14
15	16	17	18	19	20	21

Practice Makes Perfect

To fill out weeks three and four of your *21-Dinner Rotation* calendar, simply duplicate the six meals from weeks one and two. Voilà! You've just meal-planned for an entire month. Not only will you use up purchased items, but you will also become more familiar with your recipes, cooking processes, and where to locate ingredients in your store. Of course, if a recipe isn't a big hit, toss it and replace it with something new. Keep only the recipes that you both enjoy.

April

SUN	MON	TUE	WED	THU	FRI	SAT
1	2 Thai Chicken Jasmine Rice Sugar Snap Peas	3 Rigatoni w/ Meat Sauce Caprese Salad	4	5 Salmon Mashed Potatoes Asparagus	6	7
8	9 Pork Chops Blackberry Sauce Sweet Potatoes Fresh Green Beans	10 Chicken Marsala linguini pasta broccoli	11	12 Beef Tacos, Pinto Beans, Cilantro Lime Rice, Guac & Chips	13	
15	16 Salmon Salad with Asparagus	17 Spaghetti w/ Meat Sauce Tossed Salad	18	19 Thai Chicken Jasmine Rice Sugar Snap Peas	20	
	23 Chicken Marsala Linguini Pasta Broccoli	24 Beef Tacos, Pinto Beans, Cilantro Lime Rice, Guac & Chips	25	26 Pork Chops Blackberry Sauce Sweet Potatoes Fresh Green Beans	27	
29	30					

Duplicate the 6 recipes from above to finish the month.

Feel free to change-up the order of the meals during Weeks 3 and 4. You can even enjoy some shortcuts! Freeze half of the meat sauce from Week 1 and serve with spaghetti on Week 3. You've created an entirely different meal just by changing the pasta & salad.

Live intentionally

Instead of allowing the lack of a dinner plan to control you, take control of tonight, the week, and the rest of the month by planning ahead.

12 Becomes 21

April

SUN	MON	TUE	WED	THU	FRI	SAT
1 Tomato Basil Soup Grilled Cheese Sandwich	2 Thai Chicken Jasmine Rice Sugar Snap Peas	3 Rigatoni w/ Meat Sauce Caprese Salad	4 Dinner at Liz & Jeff's	5 Salmon Mashed Potatoes Asparagus	6 Filet Mignon Loaded Baked Potatoes Caesar Salad	7 Out of Town
8 Out of Town	9 Pork Chops Blackberry Sauce Sweet Potatoes Fresh Green Beans	10 Chicken Marsala Linguini Pasta Broccoli Florets	11 Evening Event	12 Beef Tacos, Pinto Beans, Cilantro Lime Rice, Guac & Chips	13 Grilled Shrimp Kabobs, Couscous, Greek Salad, w/ Pita Bread	14 Date Night
15 Shiitake Mushroom Burgers & Oven Fries, Sliced Tomatoes	16 Salmon Salad with Asparagus	17 Spaghetti w/ Meat Sauce Tossed Salad	18 Meeting	19 Thai Chicken Jasmine Rice Sugar Snap Peas	20 Date Night!	21 Homemade Pepperoni Pizza w/ Italian Salad
22 Potato & Leek Soup in Garlic Bread Bowls	23 Chicken Marsala Linguini Pasta Broccoli Florets	24 Beef Tacos, Pinto Beans, Cilantro Lime Rice, Guac & Chips	25 Working Late	26 Pork Chops Blackberry Sauce Sweet Potatoes Fresh Green Beans	27 White Fish w/ Orange Sauce, Fingerling Potatoes & Sauted Spinach	28 Out w/ Friends
29 Chicken Marbella White Rice Spanish Salad	30 Meat Loaf Panninis Tomato, Red Onion & Cucumber Salad					

Here's the thinking around my schedule. What will yours look like?

 Day One

Serve a healthy soup on the first day of the rotation (shopping day). The reason: A soup is quick to make, and you can use up the food in your fridge, freezer or pantry— the food that is least fresh. After you've shopped, unloaded, and put everything away from your trip to the store, you'll appreciate a simple meal.

 Midweek

Choose menus that come together in under 30 minutes. For nights when your schedules don't align, plan a one-pot meal. A slow cooker keeps food warm for several hours, and the leftovers can be enjoyed for lunches throughout the week.

WHY IT GOES WHERE IT GOES

There's a process to matching meals to the dates on your rotation calendar. You're setting a mood with your menu selection, so it deserves a little thought. For example, grilled rib-eye steak and Caesar salad might sound more inviting on a Saturday evening at home than Great Northern Bean soup. But how about serving that Great Northern Bean soup on a chilly Tuesday night as you're sitting in front of a fire after a hard day's work? Both meals are great, but positioning them correctly on your calendar makes all the difference in your enjoyment level—and isn't enjoyment what we're trying to achieve? Aim to bring a level of anticipation and enjoyment to dinnertime on a consistent basis.

MyTip: Avoid serving the same type of food twice in a row. Don't serve a chicken meal right after another chicken meal, or follow a rice dish with yet another rice dish, or serve spicy food after a spicy selection.

Plan to serve fresh items first in your rotation, saving canned and frozen items for later in the month.

Pay attention to the texture of the meal. Does the selection have a heavy gravy or sauce? If so, follow it with lighter fare, such as flaky fish on a spring mix salad with grilled asparagus.

Consider your time allotment. If there's a night when your cooking window is exceptionally narrow, consider leftovers or a ten-minute Tortilla Soup recipe, found on the recipe page at OurNewlywedKitchen.com

Special occasions or events are fun to plan for and break up the week. Look forward to following your tough day at work with a homemade pizza and movie night, or a hearty chili and game night.

Even though you have a plan, be flexible. Never miss an opportunity to be spontaneous, since this is one of the keys to keeping fun in your marriage.

 Weekends

 Sundays

Keep your weekend options open. Have a steak on hand for a romantic dinner for two, or if you're in the mood to entertain guests, grilled shrimp kabobs, couscous, Greek salad, and pita bread come together easily for a last-minute gathering.

Sunday brings an opportunity to open your home around the traditional midday lunch or brunch. You prepare the main dish and ask others to bring the sides. Or, take advantage of a leisurely afternoon to try a new recipe.

She looks well to the ways of her household and does not eat the bread of idleness.

PROVERBS 31:27 ESV

Essence of the 21-Dinner Rotation

Stop chasing dinner: Do you find yourself doing these two things nightly: hitting the grocery store or dining out? Choose to go out for a purpose or celebration, not because you didn't have a plan.

Take the time: Coordinating your menus with your calendar encourages a thought-out plan for the week, giving you control of your time, health, and budget. The 21-Dinner Rotation is an investment in all three.

Say good-bye to the everyday shop: With this multi-meal plan you'll shop less frequently and more efficiently, saving you effort, money, gas, time, and possibly your sanity.

Make it a routine: This system works best during the week when time is scarce. Consider planning and shopping over the weekend, and cooking dinner Monday through Thursday evenings if possible. Make adjustments according to your work schedule.

Start small: Look for 30-minute meals and focus on recipes with fewer ingredients and simpler techniques. The Food Network website (foodnetwork.com) has plenty of these recipes to choose from and helpful video tutorials. They also rank the recipes according to difficulty level.

Avoid dinnertime doldrums: The 21-Dinner Rotation was designed to eliminate dinnertime boredom, strangely enough, through repetition. Having a plan means you can avoid eating the same fallback meals over and over again.

Build confidence: As you develop and test your recipe collection, your time in the kitchen will become more efficient and enjoyable.

Shop your pantry: Before you hit the local grocer or farmers market, shop in your own pantry, spice rack, fridge, and freezer. Make sure you deplete the products you have on hand as you plan your menu and next shopping trip.

Think health & budget: If you have a grocery list when you walk in the store, you'll be less likely to reach for those unhealthy, high-calorie snacks, preservative-laden boxed products, and costly store-prepped foods—and that's good for your waistline and wallet.

Stick to your list! It cuts down on wasteful grocery spending. The only exception: staple food items on sale. Go ahead and purchase multiples in order to stock your pantry. *MyTip: Double-check the expiration date.*

Add variety: Divide your recipes by season. Spring and summer: fresh salad ideas and grilling options. Fall and winter: hearty soups, stews, and seasonal roasted veggies.

Save time: Reuse your 21-Dinner Rotation menus. This will save you even more planning time.

Elise's take on the 21-Dinner Rotation

If you're anything like me, you have the tendency to ignore your mom's advice in an attempt to find a better, more "you" way to do things. What works for her may not work for you. There's nothing wrong with having the gumption to blaze a trail for yourself. But have you ever hacked a trail through the proverbial jungle and then realized that life would have been so much easier if you would have listened to your mom? My trouble with the evening meal is one of those cases. Luckily for you, the 21-Dinner Rotation was not authored by your mother, so go for it. Trust me, if you use it you'll save yourself time, energy, and the hassle of making eleventh-hour decisions.

When my husband and I were first married, I was so excited to unwrap all of our new kitchen gadgets, organize the kitchen, and start cooking. We prepared and enjoyed our favorite meals and vetoed new recipe flops. It was fun. It was new. But then . . . it got old. The fun, romantic test-kitchen ideas eventually settled into mundane menus.

When the quick trips to the grocery became a redundant evening chore, I realized we needed a plan.

I was all too familiar with the 21-Dinner Rotation.

> WHEN THE QUICK TRIPS TO THE GROCERY BECAME A REDUNDANT EVENING CHORE, I REALIZED WE NEEDED A PLAN.

I grew up seeing Mom's monthly meal plan taped inside the pantry door. But I doubted it would work for me. I assumed it was for people with big families, with hungry teenage boys to feed, but not suited for a couple. I thought it would take too much precious time to plan for a whole month, and why would I want to plan that far in advance, anyway? Our schedule was always changing, and our plans were often spontaneous.

It was years before I tried the plan for myself. And guess what . . . it was a huge success! I was surprised by how simple it was to plan and encouraged by the results. I felt organized and prepared all month long. Dinner was no longer a nightly ordeal, but rather something I looked forward to preparing. Cooking was no longer a chore because I knew what I'd be making and that the ingredients would be on hand. We saved time and effort each evening and found some surplus in our monthly budget.

There are so many things in life you can't control. But this is not one of them. Take control now and begin forming smart habits centered on your family's dinner. It just might save your sanity. ❧

SAVE YOURSELF THE NIGHTLY STRUGGLE AND TRY THE 21-DINNER ROTATION FOR YOURSELF.

Our Newlywed
KITCHEN

• DOWN THE AISLE •

Down the Aisle

You've probably found your way down the aisle of a grocery a time or two. You can find what you need, but that's not the same as developing true shopping skills. Here are some suggestions that will save you time and money.

Always take a list: Take inventory of your pantry and know what you really need before you enter the grocery. Guessing or forgetting leads to a return trip, which is a waste of time, effort, and energy. Keep an ongoing list in your phone, on the fridge, in a drawer, or taped in a cabinet.

Don't shop hungry: If you are hungry when you shop, it's more difficult to stick to the list.

Limit shops to once a week: The more you're in the store, the more you're apt to buy items that are not on your list. The extra trip costs gas and time, too.

When to shop: If possible, shop when the store is least busy to avoid the frustration of long checkout lines and overcrowded parking. Crowded grocery stores create a sense of false urgency leading to impulse buying.

Shop weekly ads: Look online for your store's weekly discounts and plan meals around the sales items.

Know your prices: It's the only way to know if an item is truly a good deal and worth stocking up on.

If possible, shop without children or friends: Not that we don't love them, but they make for slow and unfocused shopping.

Buy in-season: Out-of-season produce is more expensive and never as fresh. Keep this in mind when you're planning your meals.

DIY: Avoid the expense of single-serving food and pre-packaged items, such as diced veggies. Do the chopping yourself.

Buy in bulk: Staple items are less expensive when bought in large quantities. Consider buying large packages of meat, rice, sugar, flour, coffee, tea, canned tomatoes, boxed chicken broth, oil, pasta, and paper goods—anything that can be frozen or stored easily in a pantry. Don't forget to invest in stackable storage containers with tight lids.

Buy generics: Store brands are usually less expensive and often packaged by the same company as the top brands.

AVOIDING THE GROCERY GOTCHAS

As you shop you'll need to be wary of the grocery store snares—the gotchas—that will entice you to purchase more than you planned on or pay more than you should. To successfully maneuver through your grocer's gotchas, make use of these insights.

Hungry yet? The aroma of bread baking and chicken frying is intended to stimulate your appetite. And it works! They know if you smell it, you'll buy it. Stay disciplined—don't fall for this marketing trick.

Flowers and produce are located in front of the store, stimulating the senses and instilling the idea of freshness. Purchasing flowers isn't necessarily a bad thing if they aren't an impulse buy, neither is fresh produce if it can all be eaten before it goes bad.

Store music is intended to slow down your shopping pace. More time in the store equals more money spent.

End caps aren't necessarily sale items. This space is often sold to companies promoting a product.

Shelf placement matters: Eye level items are often pricier. Top and bottom shelves house less expensive selections.

Sales tactics like 10 for $10 might be more expensive than if the items were purchased individually.

Buy one get one items often can be purchased singularly at 50 percent off. Check your grocer's policy.

Shopping carts You'll find some grocers have increased the size of their carts, which encourages shoppers to fill them. That's a convenience that can wreck the budget!

Unit pricing isn't always a valid indicator of value. Comparison shopping with price-per-ounce information would seem to be the best indicator of value, but many states don't regulate how your grocer labels the unit price. Compare items carefully, making sure the two items are the same size. The unit of measure listed on the shelf label should be the same as the one displayed on the package.

Beware of more expensive bulk items: As counterintuitive as it may seem, certain items can be more expensive purchased in bulk than in smaller quantities. Compare the price per ounce with a smaller package of the same product to get your answer.

Don't get clipped by coupons: Yes, everyone loves a deal. But many of the items you find on coupons won't be on your list since they are either introductory products or don't fit the way you eat. Traditional coupons require valuable "read time" to make sure they align with store policies and expiration dates. Paper couponing also requires clipping, and storing, although many stores now offer online coupons. Link the coupon to your loyalty card for extra savings. Give couponing a trial run to decide if it's worth your time and effort.

Finally, the market that earns your money and loyalty will be determined by what it can offer you. Decide which one meets your priorities.

Use these *QuickStart* options as you prioritize your market needs.

- **We're health and environmentally conscious.**
- **We have a big pantry. Buying in bulk is no problem.**
- **Convenience is critical. We're shopping close to home.**
- **Budget is first and foremost. We're saving for a get-away.**

Feel free to shop at several stores that meet your needs. See the list of market options on the next page to find the ones that work for you.

Market Options

Farmers markets offer locally farmed and harvested meat, dairy, and produce, and support the regional grower and organic farmer. The farm's close proximity to the market means less fuel is used to transport goods—that's great for the environment. Bonus: When you purchase food for human consumption from a farmers market, sales taxes may be waived, making this option a healthy, budget-friendly choice. See if this tax bonus applies to your community.

Neighborhood markets such as Albertsons, Kroger, and Walmart Neighborhood Markets offer close proximity, friendly service, and familiar faces. They are convenient if you left an item off your list and need to return to the store. They offer conveniences such as a pharmacy, butcher shop, and florist. Bonus: Neighborhood markets are going organic because they are now competing with the natural food stores.

Organic markets such as Whole Foods Market, Trader Joe's, or Sprouts Farmers Market tend to appeal to a more holistic, natural, food-is-medicine audience. The offerings aren't necessarily budget-friendly but they appeal to the health-conscious consumers. You'll find smaller carts are the norm because they target frequent shoppers.

Wholesale membership clubs such as Costco and Sam's Club offer competitive pricing for bulk foods. They also sell high-end brands of clothing, electronics, appliances, and household and health items. It's a no-frills warehouse shopping experience, requiring a membership. Pros: Buying in bulk saves money, since the price per item usually is reduced when you purchase large quantities. Cons: Specific food selections and brands can be slim since the store carries the vast array of products mentioned above. For a couple, buying in bulk may not be advantageous for many grocery items, for example, bottles of condiments might spoil before they're used up. Keep this in mind before plunking down the membership fee.

Deep-discount markets such as Aldi offer little ambience or service, but what they sell is definitely less expensive. You may have to bag your own groceries, rent a cart, and bring your own sack for toting home the goods, but the price is right.

Online grocery shopping is convenient and more prevalent than ever. After ordering online, you simply pay at the store before picking up your selections.

Home grocery delivery provided by businesses such as *Blue Ribbon Foods* can bring frozen organic meat, fish, vegetables, some prepared meals, and desserts directly to your door. Theses type of delivery businesses offer a complimentary menu-planning session. If you have the extra space, they will deliver a freezer, charging a small rental fee, but it comes with an insurance policy. In the event of an electric outage, the food is covered. They request a six-month commitment and offer a payment plan.

Make your grocery shopping journey easier. Download one of our Grocery Grab lists at **OurNewlywedKitchen.com**.

Preportioned Dinner Delivery

Preportioned dinner delivery subscriptions offer recipes with premeasured ingredients you cook, and the ingredients are delivered to your door. These companies are gaining popularity because of our busy lifestyles. Although the 21-Dinner Rotation is my answer to the "What's for dinner?" dilemma, I was curious about this clever concept. So while I was bogged down during a hectic work season, I used a coupon and gave the subscription a try. I concluded there is something to be gained from this innovative culinary idea. And who doesn't love to receive a package?

Where to Look

freshly.com	*hellofresh.com*
plated.com	*peachdish.com*
blueapron.com	*sunbasket.com*
greenchef.com	*marleyspoon.com*

Advantages

- The boxed meals were received cold-packed and neatly organized.
- The ingredients were fresh, organic, grass-fed, wild-caught, and high-end.
- The recipes were made even more enticing via a brief introduction to the origin of the dish, followed by a mouth-watering description of the food prep.
- Directions walk you through new terms, cooking techniques, and simple ways to tackle a task.
- There were no wasted ingredients, the meals served up beautifully, with pictures to show plating, and the food tasted restaurant quality.
- The meal subscription offers an option to change menu choices or skip the week altogether as long as you notify before deadline.

Disadvantages

- The cost is relative to dinner-for-two in a restaurant, minus tax and tip.
- The portions were ample, but not large enough for leftovers.
- Replicating the meal wasn't easy because it was difficult to find some of the ingredients in the grocery store.
- There is a deadline for canceling a shipment.

My Take

I found this concept to be a viable teaching tool. Consider using the preportioned dinner delivery as a way to gain cooking skills, practice timing, and learn how to plate your meal.

No matter how or where you shop, I encourage you to practice the life-changing routine of gathering around your home's table. As you continue trying out new meals, collecting recipes, and eating together, you'll establish the kitchen as the heart of your home.

I wish you a healthy, budget-conscious, and time-saving experience.

Our Newlywed

KITCHEN

· FROM THE TABLE UP ·

If the kitchen is the heart of the home, then surely the table is its pulse, for from it comes the energy, the life-giving connection, and the mood you wish to present. If it's true that we eat our first bite with our eyes, and I believe that to be so, then the table presentation is an extension of the meal. But it's so much more. Your table speaks volumes. Make it say: "You belong here, your presence is anticipated, we have a date, and I can't wait to see you again." Your table is a place of intimacy as you share your day with one another and with God as you open your hearts in prayer. Make it an unspoken message of welcoming.

The ART of the TABLE

Those who know me well know that the art of the table is my joy. I love to reinvent my table with flower arrangements, plants in antique bowls, baskets, or trays. It brings new life to the room. When changing arrangements look for unexpected vessels from around your home. Scavenger hunt in your yard or neighborhood, gathering fresh clippings of hydrangea, wildflowers, evergreen, vines, and branches. Find beauty in simplicity. Even a cluster of rooted ivy can become a beautiful centerpiece when placed in a glass jar adorned with a ribbon.

Shop end-of-season sales for deals on natural décor such as pumpkins, gourds, sunflowers, and seashells. Look for colorful linens—napkins, tablecloths, runners, and placemats—to complement the season. There's no need to purchase an entire set of holiday dishes when an accent plate will do, and you'll save storage space and money. Shop in antique stores for unusual containers to house flowers, candles, or condiments. Height on a table always adds a bit of drama, but keep in mind that you'll want to see your love across the table.

Look to nature to complement the earthen properties of your dinnerware. The soft and subtle colors of these natural elements will give a warm and inviting aura to your tablescape.

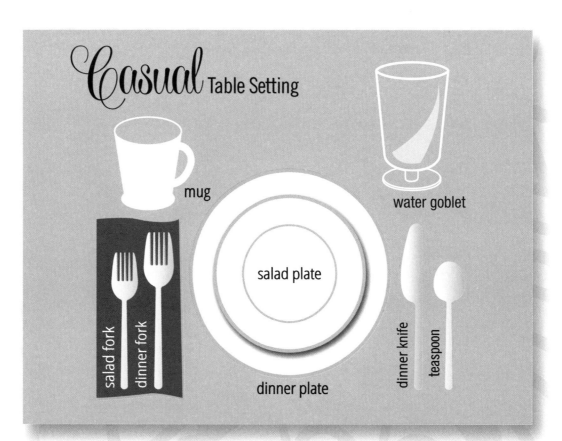

Casual Table Setting

- mug
- water goblet
- salad fork
- dinner fork
- salad plate
- dinner plate
- dinner knife
- teaspoon

Formal Table Setting

- dessert spoon
- cake fork
- butter knife
- bread plate
- salad plate
- dinner plate
- water goblet
- cup & saucer
- salad fork
- dinner fork
- dinner knife
- salad knife
- soup spoon
- teaspoon

Set the TABLE

Ah, the setting of the table. A fine pastime it is. Whether it's dinner for a small gathering or simply the two of you, it's nice to set a table with the tools everyone will need to truly enjoy the meal at hand. Believe it or not, the standard table setting was created for function, not form. Let's look at this in the simplest of terms: The more courses you serve, the more tools you'll need.

It goes without saying, start with a plate.

If you are planning to start the meal with a salad, set the table by stacking the salad plate atop the dinner plate. When the salad is finished, the plate is removed and the entrée is served on the plate below. Function!

Since 90 percent of your guests will be right-handed, the place setting is laid out to accommodate the right hand.

Utensils are placed around the plate according to sequence of use. The salad fork and soup spoon hold the outside positions, and are used during the first course(s), followed by the dinner fork (inside left) and dinner knife (inside right). The glasses are set within reach, again to accommodate the right-handed majority.

As seen in the place setting diagrams on the opposite page, the formal table involves additional items for a more elaborate dinner event.

MyTip: Set the table for the evening meal while unloading the dishwasher in the morning. It's efficient, will save you time in the evening, and leaves an unspoken message of welcoming.

It's not how you set your table that makes the event special; it's who's around it.

SET THE *Mood*

Take a break from reality and give your week a lift with the following ideas for celebrating life together.

Feeling a little romantic? Light candles.

Just want to relax and watch a movie? Set the coffee table.

Beautiful evening? Take dinner outside.

Celebrating a birthday or anniversary? Think charger plates and cloth napkins. Set out the good stuff—fine dinnerware and crystal.

Ambience: the difference between eating and dining

Dream it. *Theme it.*

Cozy soup supper

Breakfast for dinner

Mexican fiesta

An elegant evening for two

His favorite meal

Sporting event snacks

Italian Night

Grilling under the stars

Dinner&Movie Night

GIVING
THANKS

Mealtime is the perfect time to turn our focus away from ourselves and turn our hearts toward God. As we gather to eat the food that God provides, it's right to give Him thanks and praise. Everything you need to know about prayer is found in Matthew 6: 9-13. This is how Jesus has taught us to pray:

Our Father in heaven,
hallowed be your name.
Your kingdom come,
your will be done,
on earth as it is in heaven.

Give us this day our
daily bread,

and forgive us our debts,
as we also have forgiven our debtors.
And lead us not into temptation,
but deliver us from evil.

Amen

Stay connected by sharing prayer, serving and *Laughing* together, & building mutual goals.

MEALTIME IS FACE TIME

By now, I hope you've created a kitchen that works for you, acquired the tools through your registry, collected cherished recipes, and planned a healthy menu that fits your budget. By bringing these basic elements together, you've laid the foundation of an inviting kitchen, a place where you can show love to the people who gather there. The final step is to use this time to nurture your relationship. Make this your special time to reconnect after the day apart. Protect your dinnertime from disruptions. Guard it first and foremost for one another. As your family grows, this time will become an integral part of your evening routine. ⌘

Our Newlywed
KITCHEN

· GATHERING ·

SOMETHING NEW

FOURTH OF JULY

A CELEBRATION

Traveling the back roads home, I kept pace with the curves of the double yellow lines, passing cows and dewey hay fields, playing peek-a-boo with the sun through an early morning haze. My thoughts ran deep and emotions high as the events of the past weekend played over and over in my mind.

As we eagerly anticipated the three-day holiday weekend, while it held certain promise, it was just supposed to be a gathering of two families joined through friendship and marriage, a celebration of summer and our nation's birthday, and a chance to catch up on all the news—not a weekend to be written in our history books. Years from now as we relive this moment, the details will more than likely be embellished and the truth stretched a bit.

Our Fourth of July weekend began as always with hugs and hellos as our daughter's in-laws arrived. We congregated around the picnic tables with a cold and juicy watermelon and crossed our fingers as we jointly warded off any threat of rain. Siblings shared lively conversation and updates—a new boyfriend was there, another relationship started. There was talk of moves and travel, internships and school. During a lull in the conversation a quiet "Ahem" slipped from our daughter's lips as she and her husband took center stage.

"So . . . have you heard the news?" he said.

There was a brief pause as a sly grin formed on our daughter's lips.

"We're pregnant!" she announced.

A moment passed as the news was processed and siblings shared queried glances. Our group erupted into loud bursts of joy; someone spiked a watermelon like a football in giddy exuberance while others embraced joyfully. Our two families—friends first, then joined together in a family bond by our children's vows, were now sharing progeny.

Our shared excitement could not be contained.

As we all settled into the rhythm of the day—a swim, a boat ride, the lighting of the grill—something else was transpiring. Some of us noticed the clues—the new boyfriend and his girlfriend's father had been gone a long time on a kayak ride together, and as we pulled buffet potatoes out of the oven and pushed berry cobbler in, a secret was whispered: "He's asking for her hand, you know." Time stopped (as it tends to during life-changing events) but only for a moment as our attention was quickly diverted to more guests arriving just as our kayakers returned. "Happy Fourth," was shouted in greeting, we served Roy's famous barbecue chicken, and then prayed and ate as the sun set over the now still lake. After the younger set had finished the last of the clean up, we climbed into the boats. As we puttered and maneuvered through a mass of boaters searching for the best spot to observe the bright explosions in the darkening sky, I thought of my family growing before my very eyes, and wondered privately with my God, *Does it get any better than this?*

Does it get any better than this?

The next morning, over eggs and a hardy inquisition, the daughter's father shared his thoughtful response to the boyfriend's marriage request. And it's worthy of mention. He said to the young man, "What a weekend you chose to visit our families, with the news of a baby on the way. I guess you really are in the loop now, a part of us. What you just witnessed are the good times. This is the reason we stick it out through the hard times. It's not always easy you know—being a husband or wife, part of a family. It's work, but the joy of these moments together is what makes marriage worthwhile. Welcome to the family."

Hearing his words, I saw the fruit of our labor with new clarity.

Hearing his words, I saw the fruit of our labor with new clarity.

These *are* the good times. They are magnified when we share them together. And this is why we go to the trouble of building something greater than ourselves: a family, a home, a tradition, a reason to gather. As I let the news of a first grandchild wash over me afresh in an affirming moment that seemed to stand alone in time, I realized we had built a place of welcoming.

Isn't it funny how life can change with an unassuming "Ahem?"

Someone new. Cade Thomas Morris and proud Daddy.

Entertaining is one of my favorite pastimes. Welcoming family and friends into our home, deciding what to serve, and then creating inviting tables to converse around both energizes and gives me purpose. I feel a sense of unity and kinship during those moments gathered around the table. Listening to stories and sharing ideas through the warm glow of candlelight while enjoying a good meal is like hitting the pause button of life; it's a moment to relish, relax, and appreciate one another.

A PLACE OF
Welcoming

If you also feel a sense of joy at the idea of welcoming others to your home and offering them comfort, then we are kindred spirits. My hope is that you will glean something useful from this chapter. But if this is new territory for you, and you're a bit uncomfortable about gathering people around your table, let me assure you: hosting is little more than the creative offerings of a servant's heart.

In this incredible, and yet impersonal time of technology and fast-moving lifestyles, offering genuine face time is of itself a generous gesture, and critical to our well-being. If you are willing to try to host an event, I encourage you to do so. Don't let a tiny apartment, dingy carpet, or home renovations stop you from extending an invitation. Your lack of cooking skills, imperfect surroundings, or apprehension should never deter you from giving the gift of welcoming.

As you consider some of your own unique opportunities to bring people together, keep this in mind: While you do need to spend a certain amount of time and attention on the details, these events shouldn't center on food, the setting, or the quest for perfection. It's friends and fellowship we seek. Don't fall into the trap of thinking what you have to offer in space, generosity, or skill is unworthy. If you have the desire to give, others will be blessed.

Do nothing from selfish ambition or conceit, but in humility count others more significant than yourselves.

PHILIPPIANS 2:3 ESV

Why?

It's in Your DNA

You rarely need a reason to gather people together. We're built for relationship and friendship; we need to reach out and be with one another. It's part of our design, our DNA. It's the way our Creator made us.

Executing a gathering in this fast-paced age of screen-loving, career-saturated exhaustion is the difficult part. Instead of asking yourself why you should host a party, ask "Why not?"

When life is busy, I tend to plan around the expected celebrations—the holidays and birthdays. These celebrations are a given. But we also shouldn't miss the chance to gather during ordinary times—the Thursday night board game, the Saturday afternoon impromptu cookout. A last-minute get-together is the perfect setting for learning what it's like to host, and it comes with far less pressure of perfection.

Your gathering should be focused on friends, not fuss. And aren't people the reason we gather anyway?

IDEAS TO GATHER AROUND

The more creative the party idea is, the more intrigued the guest will be. This often results in an enthusiastic commitment from the people you invite. Here are a few trending ideas for you to consider.

Girlfriend's birthday party: A small coffee or afternoon tea party lets her know she is special and appreciated. Basic and beautiful, this gathering is easy to pull off with simple baked treats, fresh fruit, and a pot of coffee or tea. Go the extra mile by offering coffee flavorings or a tea service.

Bridal shower: A Saturday morning brunch is the perfect backdrop to shower the bride-to-be. A brunch allows for a slightly dressier occasion. The word alone ignites celebration. Egg dishes take center stage around other fare such as fresh fruit with dip, shrimp and grits, sausage balls, and baked cinnamon rolls. Give others an opportunity to toast the bride-to-be.

Baby shower: An afternoon luncheon offers a relaxed and casual atmosphere to celebrate the mother-to-be with care and pampering. Give her a day to remember with a lunch of poppy seed chicken, spinach salad, and strawberry cake. Fruit tea and coffee add an elegant touch.

Christmas ugly sweater contest: Ho Ho Host this fun event with a holiday buffet. Provide a main dish of baked ham or oven-roasted turkey, and ask guests to bring the sides. Now all you have to do is set up the Christmas tree and dig out those abominable sweaters.

Reveal party: This type of party allows a couple to tell the world, "It's a girl" or "It's a boy" before the delivery. It's an honor to host such a celebration, and you can do it beautifully with a dessert party. Keep the food simple, so the focus remains on the excited new family and their reveal. All that's needed to unveil the surprise is a pink or blue cake hiding under a secret layer of buttercream frosting. Milk in mason jars with a striped straw adds a little flair to your theme.

Game night: Tapas, or heavy appetizers, and fizzy beverages work well for this party. Look to your market or deli for ready made solutions, or try a few easy favorites like olives and cheese, bruschetta, and stuffed mushrooms. This is an easy way to gather friends and ensure a successful evening, as the mere mention of games sets the mood for fun.

Puppy party: After the lawn work is complete, a late-afternoon cookout is a no-hassle way to celebrate the weekend. Invite your friends and tell them to bring their dogs. Put the drinks on ice, fire up the grill, and bake up a batch of doggie treats. Let the tail wagging begin!

Many of the recipes in this chapter are simple, easy, and fun. Find them at OurNewlywedKitchen.com.

SETTING THE STAGE

Not Just Any Day

It's hard to rally a party on a Tuesday night, unless your team is in the playoffs. Everyone is still falling into step with their beginning-of-the-week responsibilities. It's far better to plan a time that guests are more apt to attend your festivity. For example, if your party is going to run late into the evening, a Friday or Saturday night is in line. Sunday nights should be reserved for wrapping-up the weekend. Think: your favorite mini-series viewing party with a casual soup supper.

Time Frame

When you have a date in mind, check with your invitees to make sure there are no prior commitments that will deplete the guest list. Be clear in communicating the start time of your gathering as well as the hour you'd like it to wrap up. If you are serving food, your guests' arrival time becomes critical. Allow a 30-minute grace period between start time and mealtime, so guests are sitting down together when the food is at its optimum temperature.

The Open House

Every now and then consider throwing a longer affair. Hosting an open house offers a casual arrival window for guests, but you still need to set a time range for the gathering, as in "We'll be around the pool from noon 'til 4:00." This allows your guests the flexibility to attend around other commitments, and the 4:00 P.M. end time frees them up to dine elsewhere. Choose food that can be left out at room temperature for longer periods of time such as crackers and cheese, cold cuts, antipasto salad, or iced-down peel-and-eat shrimp. Hearty soups and chilis stay warm for hours in a slow cooker. Or, show your guests you went all out and serve entrées of pasta with red and white sauce in chafing dishes, for no-fuss entertaining.

Theme it

By no means is a theme necessary, but when an opportunity presents itself, have some fun with it. Themes are not for the fainthearted and shouldn't be presented lukewarm. Go for it!

Once you've decided on a theme, make sure to incorporate it into your invitations, as this will set the stage for what's to come. Wherever possible, spill the theme into all areas of the event, including food and beverages, music, lighting, activities, décor, tablescapes, and party favors. Extend the fun to guests by inviting their participation in a "whodunnit" clue party, summer luau, 80s night, or other theme; ask them to wear their team jersey, Hawaiian shirt, or costume.

FOOD AND FRIENDS

When it comes to gathering around food there's a lot to be considered, but that doesn't mean it's difficult. The first point to contemplate is how each season can influence what you serve and how you serve it.

Spring begs for outdoor entertaining, so think of rooftops, gardens, parks, and porches as special places to meet. Look to what food is in season. Strawberry walnut salad, sour cream and dill potatoes, pork sliders with spicy slaw and sweet pickles make for fresh and filling fare.

Summer brings the heat, which means so can you with spicy and bold flavors. Fiestas and barbecues are a sure bet. Your grill can be a versatile culinary playground. Think Mexican street corn covered with Cotija cheese, mayo, sour cream, chile powder, and lime. A low-country shrimp boil is meant for the masses. To cool things down, gather around the ice cream churn and slice up the watermelon.

Fall leads us to the holidays with its first cold snap. From fire pits to football tailgates, embrace the changing season with hearty red-bean chili and a cup of spiced apple cider. Mirror the fall colors with baked pies of pumpkin, apple, and pecan.

Winter's shortened days find us seeking comfort in the camaraderie of others. The warmth of home is appreciated following a brisk hike or snowball fight. Cozy up around the fire with savory soups and stews. Find solace in a cup of hot cocoa dolloped with rich whipped cream, or set up a S'mores bar stocked with chocolate squares, a glass canister of marshmallows, and graham crackers all in a row.

Gathering opportunities are endless, so practice celebrating life with those you love.

A party doesn't happen without a place. To come up with the right space for your gathering, consider everything that could go wrong. Stay with me here. This exercise will ensure your event has the expected outcome or at least a backup plan.

Space Explorations

Have you left your party open to the possibility of too many guests for the space? Either narrow down the guest list or have a plan to create more room. You can let the party extend outdoors, remove or rearrange furniture for better traffic flow, or move the party to a better location, such as a park or beach. A small space with a lot of people could end up being fun in a whole new way. If you unexpectedly find your home overflowing with guests, keep the mood light by welcoming them to your "sardine" party.

What is the weather forecast? Uncomfortable conditions are the obvious dilemma. If rain is a risk, be ready with towels, umbrellas, and a backup indoor activity just in case. If your party can't move inside, have an alternate rain date in mind.

People tend to cluster in the same locations, making for poor traffic patterns. Consider your floor plan, and place the food and beverages in different areas to break up anticipated gathering spots.

Uninvited children, while adorable, can wreak unintentional havoc on a party. If there's a possibility of children coming, prepare a kid-friendly space to keep them occupied. As you provide safe boundaries for the children within your home, you'll limit mishaps and free up parents to enjoy themselves. Upside: This might be a chance to see how your husband interacts with little ones.

Aim for crafting the optimum experience, but when life hands you lemons, set up a lemonade stand.

Our Newlywed KITCHEN

· TRADITIONS ·

Traditions clothe us in familiarity, kinship, and belonging. They bring back memories, remind us of loved ones passed, and bathe us in security. They offer a connection between us and generations to come.

On a cold first day of January, we found ourselves barely stirring, having celebrated the coming new year in jovial fashion just a few hours prior. It was one of those lazy, hard-to-get-out-of-your-pajamas mornings, when the motivation to start the day was mostly nonexistent.

Perched in front of a cup of coffee, my iPhone began to vibrate. I picked it up to hear, "We're having soup and cornbread. Come in your sweats."

"We're having soup and cornbread. Come in your sweats."

Happy to relinquish responsibility for our crew's nourishment that day, I announced our plans to the family, put on my loosest pair of jeans, and headed for the door.

Once tucked inside the cozy Morris household, our melded families sprawled on large, overstuffed leather sofas to watch the predictable drone of college bowl games. As some of us dozed and some balanced bowls of bean soup on our bellies, Marie, our host, presented us with pepper sauce in a mason jar.

"Try it. It's sweet rather than peppery," she told us. "Taylor's father used to make it, but now just his brother Carter does, and he won't share the recipe."

As I tasted the well-guarded concoction, I instantly felt a sense of their family history, stories of three rascally brothers and a connection to the past. I longed for a secret recipe of my own, of goodness found in a mason jar, of food that is fussed over and then wrapped up and shared with a family story, maybe even a juicy tidbit. Suddenly, a pang of homesickness hit me, and I was transported to my Nana's green-tiled kitchen filled with the aroma of her traditional southern New Year's Day meal of country ham, collard greens, black-eyed peas, rice, and cornbread, with all of my family sitting around her table. For two decades I was force-fed that meal and hated it.

For two decades I was force-fed that meal and hated it.

But as the years took the dear ones of my childhood, and new cherub faces appeared around our table, the desire to keep the tradition alive outweighed my intolerance for that meal. And, with Nana's forewarning of "Root in or risk a year of bad luck," who wouldn't make peace with that menu? Even now, if I'm quiet for a moment, I can still hear her chortling "Don't like collards? Don't like collards? Child, where did you come from?" As I long for her and all the loved ones from those days, I recall our traditional New Year's Day meal with fondness.

As we headed for the door after a rich, full day with our friends (our new family since our daughter's marriage to

their son), I offered to return the favor and host next New Year's lunch, vowing to myself to honor and share the menu traditions of my past. I can already hear the faint grumbles over the menu from our now grown cherubs, but I'm content in knowing that someday, they too, won't be yearning to satisfy a taste bud, but a craving in their soul. Traditions connect us to loved ones past and present and maybe even bind us to those we haven't met yet. Food has a funny way of connecting us too, like stories around a kitchen table and goodness found in a mason jar.

TRADITIONS: SETTING A NEW COURSE

Maybe, like I did when I was younger, you view traditions as not very important. Often, the traditions we cherish don't resonate with us until they are missed. You may not have given your family's traditions a thought until now, but you'll probably consider them as you move through the marriage ceremony toward your first holiday together. As you begin to meld your family's traditions with your husband's, what will you carry forward, and how will you form your own?

Over the years

Over the years I've come to realize that no matter how much I dismissed the traditions of my childhood, I ached for them when they dissolved. Family is important, and I encourage you to safeguard pieces of your history and your husband's so you can pass them down along with your new traditions. You are starting a new chapter—building a new family—and it is your shared responsibility to be the keeper of the family culture. This role carries weight, but embracing it fully will result in a strong family bond.

Keeper of Traditions

So how do you go about being the keeper of traditions? Most every family has a tradition they do well, but if you can't come up with one, reflect on your family's known qualities or traits. Are your family members thought well of for their generosity, fun-loving attitude, or adventurous spirit? Maybe they're creative, sports-enthusiasts, or outdoorsy.

Look to your family's best traits to unlock some hidden traditions. For example, I'm very fond of a family that makes a point of returning home for an annual Fourth of July parade. Their tradition is centered on the design and construction of an imaginative, and usually first-place, parade float. Latch onto your family's positive attributes and find ways to incorporate them into your newly formed family.

Discover Your Past

Take time to ask and listen to your elders regarding your family's traditions and their origins. Dig deep for rich, funny, or quirky stories with specific names, personalities, dates, locations, and yes, even recipes. Be sure to give ample focus to your guy's family as well, as you proceed to uncover little gems of ancestry.

In doing so, not only will you be establishing preservation of his family history, but you are also sure to find quick favor with his side by displaying genuine interest in their ways too. Your interest in the past instills a deeper connection with your families, and when you're aware of the history you can ensure its longevity.

New traditions
COME UNANNOUNCED

And remember it's not the what that makes the tradition special, it's the who.

How Traditions Come and Go

Most traditions create themselves through happenstance when you choose to repeat a gathering. Other times, they are born out of necessity, which was the case with my family's day-after-Thanksgiving soup supper. This tradition of offering three crockpots of assorted soups began as a need to feed a brood of family in town. Regretfully, some traditions disband. Families may move away, or changes come about because of marriages, births, or the loss of dear ones. That's why it's important to appreciate your traditions. Never take them for granted, and always be on the lookout for new ones to form.

Be the Glue

So what does it take to create a great tradition? Is it time, ritual, or repetitiveness? I'd say first and foremost comes the desire and belief that traditions are the glue that binds the family. They bring us together and produce memories that last a lifetime. Whether you grew up in a home of wonderful customs, or can't seem to locate even one, having an aspiration to create them within your new family is the first step.

Be Intentional

Traditions aren't planned, they're nurtured. I tend to be the person in our family who organizes our events, due in part to my eagerness to get us all together. Aimed in jest at some of my suggestions, my son-in-law said my plans were "forced family fun." The millennials in our family

concurred. Aware they were mostly kidding, I laughed at the "FFF" reference, and then quickly tweaked my future proposals. So in an effort to steer you away from planning an occasion that is merely obligatory, I've included some factors to consider when gathering the group.

It's really quite simple when you narrow it down. Who do you want to make memories with? Start with just the two of you; simple and shared moments are the first steps to realize new traditions as you begin your life together. Grab sleeping bags and slumber under the tree on Christmas Eve, or slow dance on the balcony beneath the harvest moon. Celebrate a raise or promotion by taking each other out for dinner, or jointly whisper a shared goal for the New Year at the stroke of midnight. These suggested starter rituals can then be built upon to create unity and memories with extended family and friends—anyone you hope to share your life with through the years. Once you've selected the clan, plan an outing based on everyone's combined interests, favorite places, and events. Try to make sure there is something for everyone. When possible, include a meal or special beverage to enhance your time together.

Adopt One

If you think about it, we have something to celebrate all the time. From New Year's Day to New Year's Eve, our calendars fill up whether or not we realize it. Without really thinking about it, any of these gatherings can become a new tradition. Make them special with your own twists.

Traditions start here.
Beach getaway
Music Fest campout
Mountain trail
Volunteering
City shopping
Gameday tailgate
Backyard bash
Rodeo parade

TRADITIONS

What will you celebrate?

Look for opportunities that come around seasonally, or annually, as we tend to remember who we were with and what we did on holidays, birthdays, and reoccurring events, such as festivals, parades, and vacations.

As you venture in search of a tradition, try not to put high expectations on an event becoming a tradition. Rather, let it organically unfold.

You'll know you've started something lasting when you're asked to bring it, plan it, or host it again next year. Remember, the best traditions make themselves.

Use this *QuickStart* as a guide to formulate the who, what, where, and when, in regard to traditions. You may find you've checked more than one box. That's fine. Now, go build something lasting!

Choose your people . . .

- [ ] Family
- [ ] Friends
- [ ] Just us

What are your interests?

- [ ] Food, Art, Music
- [ ] Sports, Games, Competition
- [ ] Hiking, Biking, Camping
- [ ] Travel, Museums, Architecture
- [ ] Environment, Volunteering, Philanthropy
- [ ] Other

Where will this happen?

- [ ] Right here in town
- [ ] Pack your bags
- [ ] At home

When can you do it?

What's your budget?

- [ ] Start saving now
- [ ] Going cheap

Afterword

This book you hold was created as a result of my mission—to nurture the bride and her new marriage. As I watched divorce rates rising and families facing brokenness, encouraging young women like you became my calling, and God gave me a vision for this book. I'm honored that He has allowed me to share my stories and lessons with you. I hope you have heard my message—that it's important to strengthen your marriage by creating a warm and nurturing home.

Next to your relationship with God, marriage is the most important relationship in your life. But if you don't know God, seek Him together. From this foundation will come your greatest bond.

I find new vitality in my own marriage and family when I'm focused on loving them well through the kitchen. Whether through a new recipe or a comforting favorite, an intimate dinner for two, or a meal for a large gathering, this is where celebrations and relationships can blossom. My hope is that you make this book your personal resource as you dog-ear the pages; jot down your ideas in the margins; and slip notes, swatches, and recipes into its folds. Refer to it often. You'll find your additions to be the map of hope when the road has become hard, renewal when it's plagued with routine, and inspiration when a fresh burst of fun is needed. Remember, this book is only a guide. It's up to you to keep the fun, love, and laughter alive in your marriage.

I've always found great comfort in and around the kitchen, not only in the food that we need for nourishment, but also through the relationships and beauty found there. For in this space, every sense God gave us is stimulated, nourished, and revived. I'm praying that your marriage be renewed, refreshed, and strengthened daily through your relationship with Christ and through the heart of the home—your kitchen.

Copyright: Photo Credits

More Resources to Help You Thrive in Marriage and Life

Starting now, this could be your best day, week, month, or year! Discover ways to express your needs, embrace your purpose, and love more fully. We offer life-transforming books, e-books, videos, devotionals, study guides, audiobooks, and audio dramas to equip you for God's calling on your life. Visit your favorite retailer, or go to **FocusOnTheFamily.com/resources**.